YOUNG
POETS *New*
OF A
POLAND
AN ANTHOLOGY

YOUNG POETS OF A *New* POLAND
AN ANTHOLOGY

Lars
Musiał
Jurewicz
Czekanowicz
Maj
Polkowski
Benka
Żukowski
Boruń
Korusiewicz
Grzyb
Pawlak
Machej
Sosnowski
Świetlicki
Ekier
Koehler
Podsiadło
Broda
Sendecki
Szlosarek
Marcinkiewicz
Titkow

FOREST BOOKS
UNESCO Publishing

UNESCO COLLECTION OF REPRESENTATIVE WORKS
European Series

This book has been accepted in the translation collection of
the United Nations Educational Scientific & Cultural
Organisation (UNESCO)

Published by
FOREST BOOKS

20 Forest View, Chingford, London E4 7AY, UK
PO BOX 312, Lincoln Centre, MA 01773, USA

FIRST PUBLISHED
1993
Typeset in Great Britain by Fleetlines Typesetters, Southend-on-Sea
Printed in Great Britain by BPC Wheatons Ltd, Exeter

The publication of this work has been authorised by the
Polish National Commission for UNESCO.

A CIP catalogue record for this book is available from the
British Library

ISBN 1 85610 010 3
ISBN UNESCO 92 3 102930 4

Forest Books gratefully acknowledges the support of the
London Arts Board

for Colin Dunnan (1950–1993)

Acknowledgements

There are so many people who encouraged me to finish these translations, which began from a very modest set of four prepared for the visit by Bronisław Maj to Glasgow in 1988. I should like to think that I have been able to do justice to that encouragement, but particularly I am grateful to Grzegorz Musiał, Bronisław Maj and Robert Tekieli for their enthusiasm for this volume and advice on the selection of poets and poems. I have not always followed their advice, but I hope the contents will surprise and satisfy at the same time. I am particularly indebted to two colleagues from the Polish section of the University of Glasgow's Department of Slavonic Languages and Literatures, Beata Oziębłowska and Magda Pieczka, who read my translations with me and advised on their correctness and gave invaluable insights into ambiguities and other possible meanings. This anthology is richer because of their contributions. Some of the translations of poems by Urszula Benka were translated together with Magda Pieczka; some of the translations of work by Maria Korusiewicz were first worked on by Alexandra Earle.

After two visits to Poland, funded by the British Council in Warsaw, there did seem to be a growing correspondence between my friends' suggestions and my personal selection. This convergence augurs well for the acceptability of the collection as a representation of the current state of 'young' Polish poetry, though the ultimate responsibility for the additions and subtractions of a list with limitations must of course be mine. I assure readers that the shortcomings are only mine, and the value of the collection due entirely to the support and advice gained from friends, translators, conversations and even kindly disputes.

Donald Pirie 1993

Contents

Introduction

Polish poetry of the 1980s and 1990s represents a clear shift
in sensibility in Polish culture as a whole, and is not simply
the result of what Polish critics have called a generation's
natural 'changing of the guard'. From the early 1970s a
conflict grew between Polish society's desire to catch up
economically with the capitalist West (parallel to the intellec-
tuals' struggle for the more abstract political necessities of
freedom of speech and human rights) and the Communist
Party's determination to maintain total social and political
control. This resulted in the 'conviction poetry' of the New
Wave poets (also known as the 'generation of '68'): in
realistic, direct language they taunted the regime that the
contrast between daily reality and its 'propaganda of success'
was almost unbearable. This was classic 'opposition poetry',
occupying the moral high ground and with its roots in the
'tradition of resistance' dating back to the Second World
War, and even further back to the adulation of the Romantic
poet as spokesman for the nation in bondage.

The poetry produced during the darkest period following
the imposition of Martial Law on 13 December 1981 and
published by the enormously influential underground press,
operated as a kind of personal and collective therapy,
but soon became as mechanical as its official counterpart,
bogged down in the obligatory, conventionalised collective
statements with imagery alluding to Romantic, historical or
religious models in an emotive and moralistic rhetoric. Few
disputed that the moral victory was Solidarity's, but surpris-
ingly the 1980s turned out to be a significant watershed, as
many poets, perhaps feeling that everything permitted by the
prevailing rhetoric had already been expressed, had started
to write very private poetry, or in some cases even stopped
writing poetry altogether. This is in fact the crucial series
of questions which have confronted most East European

writers since 1989, but which had appeared in Polish culture soon after the emergence of Solidarity in August 1980: what should I write about? in what sort of language? what is the purpose of writing? why is the public indifferent? how should I confront the burden of Polish literature's traditions and preoccupations?

Because of this period of introspection poets have been able to confront the "new order" of post-Communist Poland without the complexes or illusions of earlier generations and with a direct personal involvement that draws on authentic images and textures. Underlying this there is still the moral question of 'complicity', of being an accessory, even unintentionally, to the corrupting attitudes and practices of the 'ancient regime' of the Communist state, but in the post-1989 world of personal responsibility and entrepreneurial hedonism, the poet's attention is engaged by new contradictions; a poetry has arisen in which the mesmerising upsurge of details, objects and feelings lead to a multiplication of images and metaphors until they become overwhelming catalogues and narratives in which it is difficult to locate the theme holding a poem, or the universe, together. This is the reason for the lonely spiritual or philosophical state of mind in much recent work. The tense confrontation of external objects of desire and frustration with an internalised feeling of both superfluity and exceptional insight is the essence of Polish poetry of the 1990s.

Gdańsk, birthplace of Solidarity, is one of the focal points in the poetry of the late 1970s and early 1980s, and is the starting point of the poetry collected here. Solidarity's ethos was collective (Poland's centuries-old struggle for social justice and the recognition of national traditions), but the poets who emerged round the University of Gdańsk at the same time became known as the 'New Privacy' movement, excited as they were by the post-Freudian investigation of individual imagination and personal worlds. Their work was extraordinarily diverse in form and content and as the decade has worn on it has become apparent that they were the harbingers of a revolution in Polish verse. Unfortunately, because they came to public attention a moment before the birth of Solidarity; their investigations of their own memories, complexes and aspirations seemed selfish and irrelevant in the context of the events of 1980–81, and were branded as such in both the official and underground press. Many of the poets associated with 'New Privacy' are included in this volume (Lars, Musiał, Czekanowicz, Jurewicz and Benka) and have proved to have strong poetic personalities which have survived the decade's political events and the indifference of the readers.

Krystyna Lars is a powerful poet who illustrates the essence of the new idiom which reacted against the politically one-dimensional verse of the late 1970s. Her imagination is drawn to the underside of the late-socialist state and to idealism in terminal decline; seedy hotels, late night bars, railway station washrooms, criminal characters, corrupt Party members and the urban proletariat, loitering in strip joints, waiting in queues and hanging around the foyers of international hotels. Lars piles up surreal metaphors, endless images of socialism in decay, of individual pessimism. The desire to take on responsibility, as evidenced in the poem *I Give Birth to a Knife*, or the figure of Judas Iscariot (*That Was Me*) is thwarted by the inevitable 'brick wall' which permits no change in the crumbling industrialised wasteland. Lars' poetry replaces the codes of allusion to Poland's historic struggles with the Freudian technique of free association, and so is more accessible than the conventional Polish imagery. Instead of collective aspirations and resentments, here is a voyage through personal obsessions and anxieties using archetypes and images familiar to all Western readers: trains, uniforms, illicit meetings, and suppressed feelings of guilt, clothed in arrogance and cynicism.

Grzegorz Musiał's work reveals another preoccupation of the Gdańsk poets: the sense of redundancy of a generation too young to participate in the student protests of 1968 or the development of the workers' resistance movement in 1970, 1976 and 1980. An overwhelming sense of guilt runs through the historical events and personal experiences which crowd his poems: the Holocaust, the violence of revolution, the ambivalent response to his home town of Bydgoszcz, which "deprives me utterly/ of all the other places/ open to me/ in the world." Musiał's visits to America have not resolved his personal crises of place, time or identity. America merely transfixed him with its splendid isolation, its shallow historical memory, and the peaceful coexistence of physical beauty, wealth, power and naivety, its people limited (or liberated) by thinking only of the present, while he remains imprisoned in his guilt-inducing past. Hence the bitterness of his reactions to the glamorous and famous, to Isadora Duncan, Allen Ginsberg, Günther Grass: "I cannot understand your freedom, Herr Grass". As the world heads for ever more sophisticated apocalypses and revolutions, Musiał remains detached, registering his own neurotic sensibility and emotional perplexities. His diction has been directly influenced by American poetic tradition, moving from the short line to the long, from lyrical to epic, which is a paradigm for the general realignments in Polish verse over the last decade.

The early experimental poems of Musiał's contemporary, Aleksander Jurewicz, do not contain the convictions or the certainties of the New Wave poets of the early 1970s. Jurewicz's work is torn between an internalised lyricism and a violent and horrific imagery; as with Musiał there is a strong sense of guilt. He writes "it's already happened" and yet regrets, "there was still something we wanted to say." He also exhibits the scepticism and 'faith envy' of the Gdańsk group: "I wanted to believe." Unexpectedly, in the 1980s, his creative aridity was redeemed by a return (first in his imagination) to the town where he was born – Lida, occupied by the Red Army in 1941 and violently integrated into Belorussia. The Polish population was deported in stages; Jurewicz left with his family at the age of five in 1957. Many Poles have similar biographies, leading to confusion about their identities and a sense of being disinherited from their birthplaces in the East, areas long associated with innocence and beauty. Jurewicz's writing has moved toward the recovery of these lost territories, and combines two major themes of writing in the 1980s: the child's view of the world and the fascination with the lands to the East, perhaps more 'real' than the accelerated changes of adult years. When finally Jurewicz was able to revisit Lida his memories were faced with contemporary reality and he had to write "Nothing is left from our time here".

"I suppose I just wanted to believe", says Anna Czekanowicz, whose investigations of the fragile self have gradually moved towards a directness and simplicity of style which is, like Musiał's, the result of a stay in the United States. But her earlier work is in many ways more impressive; one remarkable cycle of poems which sends shivers down the spine portrays the state of mind of the murderous wife of Mao Ze Dong, Jiang Qing. Even in a culture distant from her own Czekanowicz sees that the grandiose plans for human happiness always pave the way for the arrogant narcissism of power, the murderousness of conviction politics and the willingness of ideology to massacre millions to achieve its ends. This century has shown that the greatest threat to mankind is the establishment of man's ideal utopia, and the greatest threat to the personality the willingness to find solace in the collective. Czekanowicz asks "do you know there is no plural, just endless singularities?" a view rarely expressed in the Polish cultural discourse.

In her hieroglyphic and heremetic verse Urszula Benka shares with Krystyna Lars a taste for overpowering imagery. A sense of confinement (whether involuntary or not is unclear) dominates, and using universal symbols in unexpected, surreal collocations, Benka has created a world parallel to ours yet totally isolated. No natural human relations or sense of time are possible in this space based on self-denial and depersonalised submission, dominated by primaeval, animalist situations, fairy-tale story lines and archetypal figures: Orpheus, Charon, the City, devils, swords and mechanisms, each playing its part, and each poem a new, frustrating restatement of the narrator's imprisonment in these obsessions. Though she has lived in France and the United States for most of the last decade Benka's voyages in the unconscious have changed very little.

Surprisingly perhaps to Western readers, this anthology contains very little of the 'poetry of Martial Law', partly because it has stood the test of time so badly, essentially being cliché-ridden, sentimental political statements, too quickly translated with an aim to maintaining the West's disapproval of Jaruzelski's junta. An exception is in the rather amateurish verse of Włodzimierz Pawlak and Ryszard Grzyb, who belonged to a group of radical neo-expressionist painters in Warsaw in the mid-1980s much influenced by the desperate state of the city and people around them. Martial Law seemed the ultimate blow in an endless saga of repression, undermining their faith in love and the capacity to create beauty. Grzyb was able to articulate the pessimistic hope for a *Deus ex machina* solution, in the form of a purifying *Golden Rain* which will rinse the world clean and reveal it to be different from the grim reality of Martial Law that would not go away. In 1986, the sense of abandonment was so deep-seated that few 'professional' poets could bear to utter the nihilistic pessimism which lies at the core of the work of Grzyb or Pawlak, or in the lyrics of the punk rock bands of the mid-decade. That same nihilistic despair is evident even in more recent work: Pawlak in the 1990s writes: "No one can prevent you asking questions/but who will provide the answers?"

The idyllic, provincial environment of Kraków offered a distinctly different environment to the capital, which even before and after Martial Law has rarely been attractive to poets. Kraków has always been an important centre for poetry, and form the beginning of the 1980s, Jan Polkowski and Bronisław Maj distilled the essence of a 'new sensibility' in their work which is dominated by a transcendant search for human happiness and the contemplation of the world's complex phenomena. "Objects require no scaffolding" claims Maj, as he searches for a reliable starting point to his deliberate meditations, and finds it supplied empirically by the senses. Maj's extraordinary talent lies in the ability to admit "I am unable to transcend what I have come to know here, to desire anything other than happiness". In his fragile specificity of time and place the poet realises something too extraordinary to put into words, "at first you did not grasp the meaning of what you saw". Maj's close examination of the conscience and the surrounding world tries to reveal underlying human motives and nature's deep structures. Unfashionable during the high season of "political correctness" of the early 1980s, the stature of Maj's writing has grown inexorably during the decade, although he has all but abandoned writing since 1983, in order to dedicate himself to the literary quarterly *Na Glos* (Out Loud).

Polkowski's first volumes at the turn of the 1970s and 1980s demonstrate the truth of the dictum that the monster of totalitarianism transfixes all who live under its sway; then, going against the advice given by a secret policeman "to avoid all contact with metaphors", as Poland emerged from Martial Law, he started to write a distinctly new poetry. Caught between optimism and pessimism, his work of the late 1980s hesitates between political activism and the desire to chart new territories in poetry, and to map the numerous layers of the Polish imagination: consider, for example, *It is good that* . . . In one of his last poems (c.1988), Polkowski portrays the process of rebirth as a resurrection, and since then has entirely abandoned poetry for his new commitments as owner and editor of a right-wing publishing group, choosing direct involvement in politics rather than the distance afforded by poetic reflection.

Andrzej Sosnowski made a late debut (his first volume appeared in 1992). His starting point is different to the other poets in this volume, plugging directly into the American tradition of Ashbery and O'Hara, whom he has translated. Writing is a casual stroll through a world which is a projection of personal impressionistic preoccupations and (surprisingly) is full of pleasant experiences too. The death of a close friend stirs a passion for healthy living, which barely conceals the fear of sickness, old age and death. Sosnowski's *leitmotiv* of *carpe diem* makes him echo Maj: "Now is the time to resort to happiness". His evocative *Essay on Clouds* is a masterpiece of reflective realism written the moment before the onset of 'real capitalism'; when Sosnowski asks "what will the new world look like?", he is hoping for an open world, a Poland receptive to new ideas and influences, because "people are illuminated by what comes from afar."

Despite the ambivalence of their attitude to the Church since 1989, during the 1980s attendance at Mass, even if only as a political statement, led many poets to appreciate the texture of Biblical language and absorb its imagery of suffering, penitence and redemption. Although some resisted this new religiosity, others, like Tadeusz Żukowski, Marzena Broda and Zbigniew Machej, at one and the same time voiced the popular desire for divine intervention and yet questioned its implications, and searching for an explanation of the ultimate purpose of the 'wilderness experience' of writing poetry in the 1980s.

Żukowski's vocabulary and style are consciously reminiscent of Romantic and Biblical precedents in stark contrast to the more modernist poetics prevalent among his generation. He wrote (and then rewrote) a cycle of 150 sonnets in letter form, inspired in part by the Book of Psalms, addressed to various recipients: lovers, God, other poets, himself. He reflects on the calling of poetry, the human need for consolation and on the uncertain nature of human belief. An internal debate about the nature of man and God is presented in terms familiar to Polish readers; the nature of self-sacrifice, the requirement to set collective aspirations before the personal, the sense that the ancestors, who embody Polish tradition, are watching over (and judging) the living.

Marzena Broda's poetry is an attempt to invest the chaos she sees around her with a spiritual value, which, as in the work of all the poets in this anthology, is entirely non-institutional. She asks imponderable questions: "What truth will survive on the plains of Eden/Will time exist without us", suggesting the immanence of the Divine Principle in the universe, although she is sceptical about that Principle's motives in revealing limited eternal truths to mankind. For Broda the natural world is a place of miraculous and unforeseen illumination, but it is an illumination that is always out of human reach. Her only recourse is to list the universe's phenomena, hoping to gain an inkling of its greater design.

Unusually, the poet Zbigniew Machej comes from a Protestant background, and the textures of his poetry are as a result even more Biblical than those of his contemporaries. His meditation on the *Welcoming the Queen of Sheba* is a parable on the need for warmth and sincerity rather than rhetoric, while the hymnodic litany of *Let us spare no pains to know the Lord* reveals a communal spirituality which underpins much of his writing. The tone is predominantly prophetic and moralist; in *An Old Prophecy*, Machej gives a powerful account of the realities and contradictions of the 1990s, a 'time of changes' immediately associated in Protestant tradition with the Apocalypse, and warns of the corruption and decadence of the capitalist present. The signs of the times are overwhelmingly negative, yet Machej offers some consolation, that "love, luckily, will once more dispose its metres with unpredictable rhythms", insisting that there is an urgent need for the sincerity of a poetry of individual emotions; however, afraid of the temptations of being a 'false prophet', he is reluctant to add to the already bewildering and surreal din produced in Poland now by the clamour from politics, the media and advertising.

Many of the poets here are torn between the traditions of civic poetry, speaking for the national cause (so well represented by the master of Polish poetry, Zbigniew Herbert, much of whose verse is widely available in English), and the recent resurgence of a poetry of personal vision. A splendid poet who balances these incompatible approaches is Katarzyna Boruń. In *History* she too re-examines the real motivations for the grand gestures of the age-old Polish struggle, "they rush faster down these streets as if they were trenches/.../murmuring the words of a prayer/for their only possible reward - to die in a state of grace". Boruń indicts the constant judgment of the present according to the past and she also explains one of the most noticeable tendencies of her generation: "it will be easier for us if... we pile up the metaphors... and wrap our tongues in poetry's white fleece."

A different sort of tension between public and private is central to Maria Korusiewicz's work. She writes in two distinct voices, both of which are represented here. The early one is that of the patient suffering in hospital, a rare presence in Polish literature (suffering is reserved in traditional Polish discourses for collective oppression by alien forces). Korusiewicz speaks of her disillusionment at her body's unreliability and her reduction to a purely physical object by medical treatment, perceiving the world through the physical sensations of a body in pain and a mind full of anxieties, wanting to end the body's domination over her.

Her second voice is that of an observer of natural corruptibility - of statues and their crumbling relevance, of embittered elderly ladies, of Caesar's murder by his peers.

An irregular quarterly, *brulion* (rough copy), began to appear irregularly in Kraków in 1987. *Brulion* brought together a group of young poets some of whom were connected with the punk rock scene and who, like Grzyb and Pawlak in Warsaw, were aware that provocation and scandal was a way of attracting public attention. They were encouraged by more intellectual circles such as Maj's *Na Glos*, and at first had some success in gaining media attention by publishing pornographic and Nazi material, giving performances of their poetry in rock concert format. Very different figures publish in *brulion* and each has added new impetus to a complacent poetry scene. At first their work appeared haphazardly, but by 1990 miniature volumes of their work began to appear, crowned by the 1991 anthology *The Barbarians Have Arrived*, an allusion to Cavafy's influential poem *Waiting for the Barbarians* (1904). The brilliant but untranslatable *brulionista* poet Robert Tekieli (not included in this anthology) deconstructs and paraphrases Cavafy to describe their programme: "in the end you're/(n't we)? so/(me) sort of/solution". Because their aggressive approach, the *brulion* poets have not been universally welcomed, though they are not as 'barbaric' or 'anarchic' as they proclaim: they include restrained neo-Classicists like Krzysztof Koehler, practitioners of opaque, haiku-like lines such as Jakub Ekier, as well as post-punk lyricists such as Marcin Świetlicki.

Świetlicki's earliest poetry attacks the dehumanising effects of military service during the years of bitter resentment between regime and people (*Slupsk 1984*) and his feelings for his country are ambivalent; for him opposition to Poland's militaristic nationalism is paramount, not the struggle for liberty and democracy. However Świetlicki is less pessimistic about the 'changes' in economic and social life after 1989 than many of his contemporaries: "When I take off my dark glasses/The world I'm in is even more terrifying/But it's real. The true colours/Are creeping into their proper places." A nonchalant attitude to the Church and national tradition are also apparent in his work, and in *An Apocryphal Tale* he challenges the superficial religiosity of his fellow Poles. In his most frequently quoted poem, *For Jan Polkowski*, Świetlicki challenges the 'politically correct' but clichéd poetry of heroic resistance; the dragon (of the Party, the Communist Past, of national tradition), he reveals to be a fiction. In the simplest possible line of revolutionary change in poetry and Poland: "It's time to open the windows...and air the room."

Jacek Podsiadło is perhaps the most outstanding poet of the youngest generation. Like Swietlicki he uses direct, idiomatic, apparently unpoetic language, yet with his ability to describe the world in many different voices, he sets new parameters for Polish verse in the 1990s. Thoroughly new is his sensitivity, simplicity and positive attitude toward the chaotic complexities of life in 1990s Poland. Podsiadło uses long lines, containing endlessly changing impressions of a world impossible to encapsulate, as in his *Song of my own Warsaw*, though an objective reflectiveness remains strong: "people ...change their beliefs more easily than themselves" - in the Polish context a damning indictment of the irrepressibly collectivist mentality in these years of 'change'. Podsiadło has also written some of the best lines of love poetry yet: "To love you with words/That is all I can manage tonight."

Tomasz Titkow, the last of these post-punk poets, uses fragmented language based on the conversational style of Warsaw students. He lives in a financially and emotionally precarious world, where he has 'dropped out' in order to live a quiet life with his wife, child and friends, and write poetry to 'save myself from oblivion'. At his best, Titkow is funny and authentic in his characterisations and situations, as in his skit *Paternursal Overcare* on the conflict between the generations.

Yet another expression of the irrelevance of 'political correctness' and patriotic allusion is the resurgence of a neo-traditionalist poetic which uses Classicist images and is intentionally hard to decipher: this is the world of Krzysztof Koehler and Artur Szlosarek. Koehler uses particular places, familiar myths or literary figures as the landscape for his scenes, but they fail to solidify from the disconnected, interwoven images and yet lack the moral clarity of Zbigniew Herbert (Koehler's undisputed model). This dreamlike world of aristocratic parks and gardens, like those at Wilanów, whose significance is barely suggested, has virtually no contemporary edge and as Koeher admits "I have lost the measure of things" and he resists all temptation to provide a key to or resolution to his private images.

Artur Szlosarek, however, creates sequences of exact description which have no apparent cause or consequence linked to a very post-modern questioning of the sincerity and authenticity of what we assume to know and perceive. Though he is convinced that "At any stage you can make a fresh start", in his chaotic reality there remains a deeper sense of unease, of a coming cataclysm.

The last of these young neo-traditionalist writers is Pawel Marcinkiewicz, whose sense of dislocation and discomfort is even more pronounced. Each text adopts another style, another disguise to emphasise that we are alone to face matters of life and death, whatever any collective ethos of solidarity might have promised. Marcinkiewicz is stoical and quixotic at the same time, but even when he stresses the necessity to escape from utopian dreams, his images imply a pervading sense of longing for grand ideals and a thorough distaste for hard reality.

An utterly different aesthetic is contained in Jakub Ekier's sparse, almost haiku-like lines which are a total contrast with other *brulion* writers. His work has been praised by the Nobel prize-winning poet Czesław Miłosz for the way his compact, reflective verse concentrates on the subtleties of language. Ekier's highly-charged sequences of words remain ambiguous while suggesting unique insights which are the consequence of the logic of syntax and grammar. Yet even at such an early stage in his career, the unavoidable conclusion for Ekier may be complete silence: "on/ you will go without a word/ without this poem without yourself".

Marcin Sendecki's work also has a minimalist tone, but usually he tells a story which begins casually and then veers off into increasingly arcane events and images, presented as incomplete by his (ab)use of the semicolon. He writes happily of the changes in Poland in 1989 that "it will be a holiday, and we will eat/ cakes!", or more impatiently, in frustration at the delays "It's certainly too early, but/ when is it likely to start?" In the most successful poem of this cycle, *Looking Down*, the field of vision gradually narrows from the view from the balcony of a flat on a housing estate to small details, and "life - put off until some later date - folds up/ into a single lump and fits in an inside pocket."

So where are this new age and its poetry heading? Has poetry found new, relevant themes and forms which can attract readers again? American poetry of the 1950s and 1960s, especially the work of Ginsberg, Ashbery and O'Hara, translated and discussed with enthusiasm, has been a significant influence on the new generation. The academics and writers, previously in opposition or emigration, like Miłosz, Błoński, Barańczak and Zagajewski (and even the Russian Brodski), have become a new establishment, and lose no opportunity to give their opinion on the current state of literature. Miłosz has been playing a very particular role, in suggesting that the way forward for Polish poetry lies in the enigmatic distillations of expression typified by the classical Chinese and Japanese poets.

The early nineties can be seen as similar to the immediate post-war period (1945–48), with the same need to rebuild a devastated country coupled with enthusiasm for a new economic and political system which promises radical improvements in standards of living for the majority of the population. The need to confront a fast-changing world and find a new language in which to discuss its realities, dangers and values is overwhelming. There are also some similarities with the period immediately after the First World War, such as in the new found sense of liberation from the themes of the past, and the attempt to depict the present irreverently, leads many poets to experimenting with contemporary language and attitudes. The shifting subject matter, the sense of moral anxiety and spiritual hunger, together with the fear that democracy might mean little in the new harsh political and economic reality, is an undercurrent in much of this writing.

Recent poetry, then, has yielded a rich and varied range of responses to the instabilities and uncertainties of this period of rapid, often incomprehensible change. Though this selection of poems may reflect a period of transition rather than a new poetic aesthetic that is the expression of a very different Polish society, it is surely also true that authentic, convincing poetry is always located in the transitional and unstable, rather than confined by the predictable. The poems collected here as *Young Poets of a New Poland* speak with the authentic voices of real 'singularities' and their very sensual experience of what is more than a New Poland – it is a New World.

Donald P. A. Pirie   Glasgow, 1993

Linguist, translator and critic, Donald P. A. Pirie was born in 1956. He studied Polish at the School of Slavonic and Eastern European Studies, London University and also at Cambridge and the University of Lublin in Poland. Since 1984 he has been Stepek Lecturer in Polish Language and Literature at the University of Glasgow.

Krystyna Lars

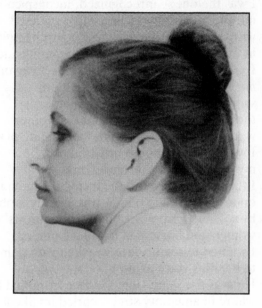

Born in Ełk in 1950, Lars studied Polish at the University of Gdańsk and was closely involved with the young writers in the Wspólność group. She contributed to the local magazines *Litteraria, Punkt,* and *Autograf;* she is the co-founder and now editor in chief of the quarterly *Tytuł,* also based in Gdańsk. Since the late 1980s Lars has had her own programme on local radio, devoted to cultural and literary themes. Her first poems were published in 1980, and in 1981 a volume appeared entitled *Ja, Gustaw* (I, Gustav, Gdańsk). It was followed by *Chirurgia mistyczna* (Mystical Surgery, Bydgoszcz 1985) and *Kraina pamiątek* (The Land of Souvenirs, Gdańsk 1991).

That Was Me

I was the one who betrayed Him in the garden
I was the one – unrecognized, inconspicuous, unlit
not the one who was later justly indicted
with my face in the darkness, a torch in my hand
in the midst of the screeching chanting and calling
I was the one who quickly slipped away unobserved,
not him, – Me, the mobile phantom
sailing silently behind the soldiers,
the disciples, the scribes and the women
who watched the fire from their hiding places
I was the one who silently branded
my mark onto his forehead
I then skirted around the incident, trailing at a distance
on towards Skull Hill – it was already mobbed
by soldiers, cripples, children and priests
women and horsemen holding banners
I wanted to see his face wracked with pain
to hear his voice again
His was the same face, the face from that town
where in an empty street, curled up like a wounded animal
I had gasped for breath in my agony
He had wanted to lay His hands on my shoulders
to pass His fingers over my eyelids
He had wanted to take away my pain
I knew He was capable of that
He could have done even greater things
But I had recoiled, suddenly pushed him away
I already knew then that he was waiting for me to
                                        forgive Him
But I could not trust him, so I watched silently
with impassive eyes devoid of tears
I was the one who passed the stick that snapped
                                        over His head
I was the one who shouted: crucify Him, crucify Him
followed by the mob, the tramps and the children
I wanted to see his face wracked with pain
His hands pierced, to hear the hammer slam down

I wanted to see it, I wanted to hear it
for pain, for death, for the agony of menstruation
for the fears that never wish to leave us
for the lingering anxiety, for the screaming desire to escape
I wanted Him to feel the sudden jerks of a child inside Him
– my jerks, summoned up for an instant from the void

The Corner Room

In this hotel, right in the heart of the city
at night
as she came in, suddenly losing
her reflections in a dormant mirror
that sucks in the interiors of rooms
deprived of name, breathing or dream movements
that can draw such images into its deepest core
like a ribbon pulled from my hair
a maelstrom of cables thrown up by some undercurrent
onto the surface of the hall's parquet
suddenly shrank back before her steps like a living plant
My sister had no faith at all in my eyes
from which she had been banished
but despite that, I sensed in the corridor's stillness
the presence of a woman, who had been conceived here by
                                        the two of them
in this hotel in the very heart of the city
at night
It was only at that point that my hands abruptly woke up in
                                        the pitch black
and my half-opened mouth
could not accept the consecrated host of the air
It was only then that I suspected
why I was here
in the corner room
next to the quivering lift shaft
at the top of this building
which slowly branches out into the darkness

Hotel [fragment]

Men stand beside the white wash basins stamped with
                                    München v. Blitz
with sullen expressions on their faces and scars on their
                                    forearms
walls are covered with oak panels and hint at the nearby
                                    woods
where young men from the evening train loiter with intent
they sway girls to sleep who have only dropped in for a while
to touch up their make-up which is pointless actually when
                                    swimming
upstream with bellies displayed while negotiating the toilet
                                    articles in the waters
that belong to the men poring over mirrors
smearing balm over their gashed necks when you sit
on top of the tumble-down bedding it is morning and
the river flows past the window exhibiting its insides
as gentle as the traces of a woman's lips on a glass with a hint
of lymph on the edge
Beyond the wall a woman is submerged into an enamel niche
she has pearl eyeballs and defrosted fingers and she swims
in the arms of a young man from El Alamein
who has a dark face and a purple bruises under his arms
water runs over the edge of the tub, its sounds recall
the faded pages of the reports written by the hotel
                                    proprietress
who fills the violet ruled lines with an immaculate script
composed of the trademark emblems Hogar Genevius Imiels
which no one can decipher any more
The restless men suddenly busy themselves
at the sight of the crippled porter his face full of
the raggedness of geranium petals a boy with stiffening
                                    hands
disappears in the direction of open windows the taste of
                                    freesias
dozing in his mouth when the red brim of a hat
calms its persistent rocking on top of a bed of nickel

and narrowed eyes follow immobile hands the corridors are
still
a white shoulder is suddenly bared by mist rising from the
river
sad smiles wake up in creaking brass bedsteads
and the marble density of veins is carved out by a razor's
brisk slashes
which illuminate the attic room for an instant
where a recently arrived guest now blocks
the view through the brown unwashed window with his old
jacket

Cariatids

The wounding glassy shards of evening rain
thud down heavily like leaden bullets
onto the surface of the water tense with a pain
that quivers airily over my head

Ahead of me women stand in monotonous shadow
with their swollen black bodies
bearing fruit under their hearts like red jelly-fish
merging into the slimy darkness

Their feet are immersed in the leaden gloom
pierced suddenly by a sharp shaft of light
the earth's stirring black lips draws all things into itself
hidden underneath the steel plates of rusting wrecks

And only the water mutely absorbs
their breathing captured as white bullets
injecting the billowing streaks of transparent blood
into the cooling ocean's open veins

Black Uniform

This black uniform like an empty banner
fluttering silently over the smouldering rubble
is covered with death heads cast in silver
with a broken cross hung on a red ribbon
it was waiting for my stripped body
breathing in water through its dead mouth

I sensed how in the silence of a stagnant sea
it stealthily slithered up onto my arm
quickly rushing like a slippery lizard
it crawled along my jaw enveloping my neck
it was cold, filled with an echo's darkness
like a black tunnel in the open air
breathing in through the body which only consumes

So I will now have a living skin
which was never possessed by
my two mortal enemies sitting sleepily
at the right hand of the father who is as
unmovable as the sea when anaesthetised

Giving Birth to a Knife

My body, unruly, tired and sleepy
slowly rolled through the streaming depths
grazed by the slippery fingers of eels
and kissed by the breath of overweight jelly-fish

In the middle of the night, on a dead river bed
within the alternating currents of clear blood
your knives slowly penetrated between my hips

There was no child within me
at the tangle of the arteries
There was no heart inside me
that could pump in or out

The knife lived in a black sea, in a cradle of blood
it lay huddled up inside me like an embryo
it exuded one unique transparent tear
and slowly it inhaled darkness

City

The most difficult thing is to believe in a transparent face
at night it is brave, by day swollen with that terror
hidden silently beneath the faces of the living
like the white light under the eyelids of a shadow

The most difficult thing is to believe in a crystallised word
ringing out lightly in the air's azure glass
swaying cautiously between our hands
like the roll-call of the dead in an unknown language

The most difficult thing is to believe in an airborne city
which is like a white body of streaming brightness
opened out with light on the edge of the sea
and which is deeply wounded by the storm's battle axes

Public Baths [fragments]

II. Voice

Women in a red waiting room can sense a dark frostiness within the tiled floor beneath their feet. They carefully examine their own footsteps which disappear as fast as the traces of breath on a pane of glass. They are calm. They cannot yet discern any pale scars that result from difficult births. They concentrate sleepily on newspapers soaking with damp. They count copper coins.

Suddenly their skin wakes up. It recoils as if in contact with fire when they hear the voices of old men slapping each other on wet thighs beyond the partition walls and they reveal their eyes underneath reptilian eyelids. At that moment their skin is crammed with memories of childhood. It remembers a scalding much as it does painless glances and gashes.

The skin trembles.

IV. Meeting

The white lingerie embroidered with green flowers has been ripped off her, so too has the belt from her hips and the light gold dust off her shoulders... She is no longer wearing a garland. Or even the thin pigeon down. Or breath. Someone's lips flutter off. Her cut hair lies strewn over the tiled floor. She waits.

Behind the partition wall a young man with a tin numbered tag on his chest is washing his hair. Inside his closed eyes naked women sing out. Underneath the skin of his hand the memory of a touch swims about. Inside his mouth the taste of a pink tongue is aroused.

Soon they will meet. Lying on an enamelled chair beneath the mirror is a recently cleaned gun. A lead bullet waits in one chamber of the gun barrel.

VIII. An Unusual Photograph

The boys throw glossy pictures around. Their fingernails have been bitten back until they bled. The sleek paper depicts bare intertwined branches – whose leaves have been burnt off by human breath. A fistful of ash passes from hand to hand. Trees have no roots, they do not know their proper place, they live above the ground. Dreaming is their oxygen. They lose the pruned measure of the apple tree. Instead of bearing fruit, wolf-berries scorch their bark. Under half-closed eyes there rises that hatred of one's mother and father. The fear that women are merely an Arabesque decoration that they will never lay eyes on.

The Guillotine Speaks to Danton

"You have no idea how dull bad theatre can be, Danton. When I am raised high, I can see a thousand eyes fixed on my glistening blade. All hands are clammy. Their thighs tremble. The idiots swallow to reassure themselves that their own jugulars have not been sliced. That's all they can think about. They only see the edge glint, the release, the descent, then the blood, the wet tufts of hair on the neck and then the basket full of yellow brains.

I really ought to be invisible. Cut from the air as if it were glass. Then the heaven of our Idea would shine out over the entire city, and transparent blood would flow down into human bodies transforming them all into white marble.

I really am the supporting strut of the Great Cupola that separates the world from the darkness outside.

Do not tell me your name again. I will not remember it anyway. Tilt your head to one side and look straight at the mob through your glasses."

The Last Compartment

All I can do now is run. I can see them down the end of the corridor. They are following me. They release the burning feathers of swallows out of their hands. Black flames wheel through the air. They settle on the velvet handrests. Icicles tremble in the passengers' hair. Frost on the eyelashes. Eyes of uranium. Phosphorus. A large pane of plate glass opens at the touch of a fan. One woman with a round face has wooden hands but no eyes. A steel point juts out from the wrist. Pearls shower down from a torn necklace. A froth of crowns frames a pair of breasts on display. A ruby cross . . . Damp roses . . . Fog . . .

They are coming closer. The skin on the walls ripples under their breath. A great shimmering lake of eczema flows out onto the damask hills. Leukemia, submerged all the while, swims through the interior of the mirrors. Her eyes are closed. Slippery lilies surround the lake's open black palm. Quicksilver lamps hung from the ceiling suck in poisonous air. A hiss. Waterfalls of fire. The sound of dresses being torn. Silken flakes tumble off shoulders . . . The hourglass buzzes like a beehive in flames.

The passages between the carriages are full of blood. Inside the windows' double panes dead insects shift. White knives of air cut through the darkness. Viaducts jump across the roaring lakes . . . The moon . . . Slit clouds . . . A scream . . .

God is seated in the final compartment. When I walked past he lifted his newspaper. I could not catch sight of his face. Red headlines swimming in blood rose up over a finger on which he wore a silver ring. Stars were spilling from his cigarette.

Grzegorz Musiał

Born in Bydgoszcz, Musiał studied medicine at the Medical
Academy of Gdańsk, where he also became involved with the
Wspólność group and Maria Janion at the University of Gdańsk.
His first poems were published in the mid seventies, but his
first volume of poetry appeared in 1978 entitled *Rewia* (Revue,
Gdańsk). This was soon followed by *Kosmopolites* (Gdańsk 1980),
Listy do brata (Letters to my Brother, Gdańsk 1983), *Przypadkowi
świadkowie zdarzeń* (Chance Witnesses to Events, Warsaw 1986),
Berliner Tagebuch (A Berlin Diary, Kraków 1989), and most
recently *Smak popiołu* (The Taste of Ashes, Bydgoszcz 1992). In
addition to these volumes of poetry, Musiał has also produced
three semi-autobiographical novels and is an enthusiastic and
accomplished translator of American verse including all of Allen
Ginsberg's work.

Generation

to my friends

so we set off
to the sound of hobnail boots
and our voices ring out far and wide –

so we keep coming back
on a winter's morning
tapping and knocking
just not the same people any more

with frost-bitten hands
with a lump in our throats
with hearts ready for flights of fancy
some of us were in the front line
we still keep torn banners under our shirts
there still remains a little warmth and although
more cruel we are less
arrogant
yet our world thrashed like a dog
and quiet as only mothers can be
wanders aimlessly through the ravaged skies

as each second passes we are
one less every moment
we set off tap
knock
and our voices ring out far and wide

October 1981

Grzegorz Musiał

Accidental Witnesses to Events

accidental witnesses to events
were passing here purely by chance
are witness to events
where they are out of their depth

accidental witnesses to events
attribute either too much or too little significance to them
rarely getting the point of hope or bitterness
only they remember the colour of the victim's shoes
or that he was wearing a ring on his finger

let's not ignore these accidental witnesses
only they can tell
who is pulling the strings of the puppet monarch
how many hands are reaching for the crown
and who is watching it all from the wings

August 1980

Isadora Duncan Dancing in a Red Scarf, 1918

how was I supposed to know
that red is the colour of blood
they told me
that it would smell of lilac
someone even slit his wrist on a razor
actually I didn't feel a thing
the scarf wrapped itself around my throat
in a flash

how was I supposed to know
that red is the colour of death
they always applauded
once they had put down their guns and knives
when I stood up in the open-topped car
they sang out
though it was more like a roar –
or a groan –
and I threw my arms up into the air;

I can't remember any more maybe
they were already dead
when with a vicious smile they carried me down the street
their women dancing and clapping their hands
and newspaper-sellers running past us heralded the advent of
death

December 1984

A Lady in Waiting Gives Evidence

I was particularly frightened a revolution might take place
when it did happen
I went and hid behind a screen

I saw how they knocked the clock off the mantlepiece
how they danced on the smashed crystal in their huge boots
I watched as they pulled down their trousers
and left foul piles of brown excrement
on the empress's dresses

they found me when I whimpered
the scene, you must admit, demanded that at least
they raped me slowly, finally one
skewered my breast with a Chinese parasol

now at least that is all behind me
I don't even care much you won't experience
the same relief as I did: revolution is a most
agreeable dormition
for a lady in waiting dressed in satin beside
a broken down door

January 1985

The End of the World at Breakfast Time

In they walked – and the banter and bitchiness stopped
the guests froze with their forks still raised in their hands
the lady of the house opened her mouth in an amazement
                                        beyond description
but they did not let her utter a word

The end of the world can sometimes be the front-door bell at
                                        breakfast
though it is best recognised by scuffles and raucous laughter
but even death's disseminators expect better manners
so now they slip in more discreetly than ever and leave no
                                        tears in their wake

And as usual they ask some poet why he didn't shout in
                                        time
like peacocks scream in the garden during a ball under the
                                        light of paper lanterns
he is the only one who recognises the extinction of an entire
                                        generation on its face
as eternity's cold breath brushes against his temples

April 1984

Lonely Men

we live right
over there next to the black eye of
the lake we don't know
our own names

we meet at night-time no questions asked
no advice given
like joyless fish without
animosity karol szymanowski
jean genet jarosław iwaszkiewicz
handsome nameless under an
unresponsive sky
arms bleed and Veronica's veil watches us with
no anger and
no hope

Oh Greece, Greece why have you done this to us
arousing us in among the olive groves
in the arms of shepherds who had once been gods –

the skies have blasted open and
for a long time were left charred
we cried for the ashen
Earth we were persecuted
by the men on the street's sneers
the cackling of their wives

we live right
over there next to the black eye of the lake a pair of
unseen men with features darkened by time

among the trees
which are laden with
incomprehensible warnings

water lilies whisper
when jostled by fish snouts

May 1981

21

Emigrants

where are you now my friends
I love you all and still
I have made no effort to relive those good times
to giggle at our voguish in-jokes
do not question a leaf's deep-set veins
what it all means

where are you my enemies who
I needed so I have now stopped
understanding the inanimate platforms
are silent the hated
dawn telephones dead
animals no one for
better or
worse gives me any answer

I examine my face in the mirror
I am inhabited by two
twins both dead
as alike as two drops of water
bitter tasting
identical

December 1984

This Place

this place.
this is where I am growing. this is where I can sing.
this is where I try. where I lose
this place. not the table. not
the chair. not even
this house.

those people.
this is what they trust. this is where they are waiting.
these are the windows from which they keep watch over me
day after day.
a recognizable coat. a familiar walk.
this is the door I knock at every day.

this place.
deprives me utterly
of all the other places open to me
in the world.

*   *   *

I am so sick
oh America of dark sycamores lining the streets
of swings floating on white porches at the front of houses
of the smell of coffee and toast which remind me of holidays
                                              in Jaźwin;
a nun of simple farming stock holds a microphone in her
                                              hand
shouts good morning and hands hold
and even arms embrace

Handel's Messiah
piped through twenty-three rooms of the Iowa Creative
                                    Writing Programme
typewriters tapping on a Sunday morning
novels of genius by order
of the United States Information Agency
small dark-haired Mary
the martyrdom of office girls
checking who's in class
is Dostoevsky here today?
what about Proust? and
de Beauvoir? she's gone for her blood test oh America
we conceal from you
the prophets of the Old and New
in religion's hollow core
but even there
the air-conditioning rumbles on
and prevents us from dreaming of you;

I do love you after a fashion
you a Jewess of Budapest who translated
the raptures of St Teresa and St John of the Cross
the Pope smiled made a sign what are they going to do
the Jews have been sent to an alternative heaven
with their heads shaved holding small scrolls of the Torah
inscribed on birchwood parchment in their hands on their
                                        way to the ovens;
I am sick

24

in love with sycamores and concrete avenues along the
                                                    riverside
for a Spanish boy who says "hold out your hand" to me
admit love don't hide tears
down by a slender box pretending to be the UN building
among the lavender bushes behind the low hedge
students turn over from one side to the other reading
                                                    textbooks
I am sick America this love
is a sickness and there is
no cure

Iowa City, September 1988

An Introductory Conversation Between Writers from Eastern Europe

I cannot understand your freedom Herr Grass
and what's even worse I don't understand myself
in you there is something watery something sharp
in you there is something fishy and something fiery
we were both extracted from mud from nipple and from

womb;

so we cut open the Earth sensing
her defenceless heart
looking for love I find hell
you are looking for the frontiers of hell that Soloviev

detailed

but all of it is fabricated my hell
your fake flames
and even the blood that runs
when you slit your wrists;

people were murdered in my country
until transformed into one ultimate human being
how can I walk the earth that trembles and groans
how can my face not ache I strike it with my open
hand and I feel the tears in heaven's eyes – everything is
a lie and that one single truth
saved Europe: I can feel inside my
heart a jagged stone
I crouch down over my agony
which is raw stone

September 1986

Poem for Allen

Allen that isn't you
a one-thousand year old rabbi embraced by a velvet armchair
on the third floor of an apartment on Chłodna Street
next to a lamp that my great grandmother remembers

we talk we move our lips
in English French you wrote of your father a real mensch
                                                            who
are you an old Jewish queen from the Bronx or an old
                                                        Jewess
from Warsaw we drink have some sandwiches the expected
props rubble all around a scream a hand which scratches at
                                                            flames
in his fine khaki uniform over you a gun held to your head
                                                            what
right do we have to a wild cruel adolescence, Allen?

we descend into dreams
I can see a Jewish boy in his skull-cap
you are that boy with your hands raised high
a New York gentleman with a small dog
handsome athletes rob passers-by in Central Park in the
                                                        evening
that's where Naomi died
on one of the lunar meadows where we wander
dreaming of bridges and stone towers
embracing that boy in his cap repeating "you too
will enter the fiery furnace";

oh Allen Allen oh poetry
a Tasmanian does not exist in each person the charred core
                                                        of our Earth
the millenial Schvul Avrum in Odessa or maybe even Lvov
not every hand like yours searches for matches on the
                                                        tablecloth
not everyone's eye is smaller than the other

not everyone recites
for hours on end the poems
of the dead Hassidim

Kerouac Cassidy
the handsomest fall
it's evening now Allen
under the ghetto's cold rain we will heed the bones
and the stones clenching our hands tightly trembling
beneath the sky's furious searchlights

October 1986

Aleksander Jurewicz

Born in 1952 in the village of Lida in what was then the Belorussian Soviet Socialist Republic, he and his Polish parents were repatriated in Autumn of 1957. Jurewicz has published a large number of volumes over the years, *Sen który na pewno nie był miłością* (A Dream that was Certainly not Love, 1974), *Po drugiej stronie* (On the Other Side, 1978), *Nie strzelajcie do Beatlesów* (Don't Shoot at the Beatles, 1983), and *Jak gołębie gnane burzą* (Like Doves Chased by the Storm, 1990). Jurewicz has also published two novellas, *W środku nocy* (In the Middle of the Night, 1980) and *Lida* (1990).

The Interiors of Our Homes

The interiors of our homes
where we return after
failed meetings with
friends of years ago
Where we page through their old
intimate correspondence
for ages they exhaled the warm
scent of springtime
The interiors of our homes
where even memories dry out like
washing or sausages Because it is easier to
return to them since death has ordained in them
a meeting before the birth of your son
to a woman at that moment unknown who tries
to run attracted by sex and an open volume of
Dostoevsky Where we pull the curtains across the windows
before dawn discovers us hunched over
a still blank sheet of paper lying on a stained
table top In our homes In
our houses of ill repute Houses of untroubled
youth In our railway stations from which no
trains depart but where only
childhood's long-abandoned dogs still call

Haemoglobin

without even disturbing our skin set hard against
the rubble of a demolished house we hum a fleeting
song over the crossroads
in haste we top up our fear glands
because when you wake up you will only see the sky
though a line of verse will be torn out of context as if
in an emergency as if a razor blade
thrown on to a hospital bed muddling
a green meadow with an empty playground
anticolo jazz with a prayer
a manuscript not yet dry with extinction already in the eyes
the fear that will one day be condemned as an error of
                                        judgment
a door handle with a gas tap
for when you wake up someone else will be shouting
a blank space between the window and the bed
a rusted nail left after a picture was taken down
a door slightly ajar

An Application for an Extension of Life

We're still here
Living among these shabby
walls furniture washing
Although we're only really chasing violently
after our own profiles And yet
we will die slowly in the back rows
of a cinema during a morning screening
We're beautiful people because we have been redecorated
                                        yet again by
despair with wind by sudden death with lyric
poetry We will slit open up the stomachs of
our womenfolk reviving them with caring
punches In the spitoons of the clinics
the cramped offspring of our fears
will slowly decompose
And this will continue as if we had been told in confidence
how to live It crept from the bowels to the brain Perhaps
someone else said: "I am as lonely as Franz
Kafka" to his friend
Franz Kafka Wait While
bitten by our own lips Suffocated
by the nymphomaniacs and old men
brought back onto the square Between the department
store and the puppet theatre
From where it is easier to get back alternately
gnawing at the asphalt scratching at the walls She who is
our contempt Mother with her arms growing
into the table A letter sent to *poste restante*
Perhaps they'll locate it somewhere They'll return it
After all we have the right to rendez-vous

Aleksander Jurewicz

Not in Time

to Leszek Rybicki

We didn't get here in time.
We got here too late.
No one is looking at us.
No one recognises us.
Even though on the table there are appetisers and
vodka is served – we have arrived too late.
We thought there was so much left to do here.
That they were only waiting for us to get here before starting
and it's all happened already.
They didn't even have time to dig
us a communal grave.
We wanted to leave them so much pain.
So many uncompleted words,
unmarked walls and exhausted hope.
There was something we still wanted to say . . .

Obviously someone got the dates wrong.
Perhaps he misread the address of that street over there.
So here we stand with tightly clenched fists
deep in our pockets and in a daze
we focus on the girls sauntering past us.
No one is watching us.
No one recognises us.
And so here we stand not marking time,
not counting the days.

1952

Our incompletely dreamt young years
torn from their bed one night
Leaden clouds above us
Women no longer long for us
No farewells and no returns
In shabby sweaters over bare bodies
Dead birds accompany us
and the emptiness of streets once so very much ours
Our young years are overgrown with grass
The white stones of skulls full of
bullet holes with which our
as yet unborn children can play
Those young years whose dream was interrupted
And wrapped in a grey sheet
Passers by do lean over the edge
The empty pit with corrosive lime
There is so much space here for those to follow
The agony of others is just about to begin

Aleksander Jurewicz

Suddenly

But we are still alive my dear,
we are still alive.
          W. H. Auden

What is the act of writing if with that same hand
numbed with terror and cold
you tie your very own
noose under your chin?
As if with that writing you wanted to silence
the knocking on a door now belonging to someone else,
as if sweating in the middle of a nightmare followed open
                                                        eyed
you struggle with the window handle
wanting to reach the slippery sill,
as if it were you who hung crucified
by the last sinews
of this town's deadly silence . . .
But then someone must say it
after all we cannot just leave
an empty space after we've gone –
let us leave at least
some sign in the air
some unintercepted coded missive
We surely can't go on like this forever:
within these walls prisoners
of our own fear, sick with some
imagined qualms of conscience
in a sleepy house in the middle of the night
night which magnifies each and every shadow on the wall
and exaggerates every whisper
to a final scream.

From window to door
on tiptoe
at the age of thirty
I want to believe that everything is
still ahead of us,
that during the best years of our youth

it was not for nothing that we wasted
talent, strength and sperm
that none of those empty rooms ever existed
despite the evidence of the ravishing times of those
who stayed here before us
(and where we waited for some miracle to happen),
that we never had any
left overs of the free soup stolen
from the student canteen,
I want to believe that in more than one
undisturbed dream we will be running
down the middle of Grunwaldzka street
holding up the Beatles' farewell album
and this main street will not reveal itself
to be a field of blood,
I want to believe that now walking
from window to door
I am waiting for you and it is not out of fear
that my heart beats so violently
at the sound of the approaching lift
I want to believe that I am not writing my final
poem from the Dead City this winter night
wrapped in this old overcoat
which had hosted a feast for the moths,
that this is still the same city
in which much as before
we still cut our fingers when slicing bread
we air our appartments, we write letters
we point out a solitary tree to our children
from the window, with a sense of
disillusionment we stroke the dog –
It was not so long ago:
leaning across the table
poring over a poem just begun
we did not speak of poetry
as the last safety plank
or that we could not sleep
at night because of the poetry
that we shouted out during public readings
or quietly whispered

to the occasional girlfriend,
we did not think about poems
which will slowly kill us . . .
We believed in those few words
which have the power to save,
we still believed in
the sun, blood and ground . . .
Now on unsteady legs
we walk down the streets of our accelerating
youth with something burnt out
deep inside and in vain we look for
words which conceal no
horrors or falsities
we are still walking
with empty hands
unable to
firmly grasp hold of the air.

*

In spite of
the as yet unread judgments
on our defenceless poems
for the days which we will not
be able to live through,
for our easy faith
and the faith of our children,
for the fist which we will not raise,
for all that is trodden underfoot:
Do not lead us
Never lead us
and do not take away the memory.

1981–1985

Lida

In memoriam: my father.

I.

I am still five years old and wearing
a sailor's suit
The last repatriation train
is patiently waiting at the station
No one gets onto it
There is no one crying on the platform
Father has got lost somewhere with our Singer
sewing machine wrapped up in canvas
Mother isn't clutching that picture of the Virgin
Mary of Ostra Brama beneath her arm
The early departing migratory birds are inaudible
silencing as they do the children's squeals of
"I don't want to go to Poland . . ."

The station at Lida is empty and sleepy
as if the plague had even reached here
although no general alert was imposed
no bells were rung
no rats ran down the street
September begins to exchange the kopeck
leaves of specific trees
In front of the station is a lorry
from which no one emerges
it does not unload goods
A man and woman with a five-year old son
sit in the lorry transfixed by the distance
which they do not have the strength to cross
as if they were waiting for a twist in their fate
or for a photographer to come along

II.

But here comes the train and the ground
moves from under their feet
The shouting and crying of those who

38

will remain here forever
and those who must leave
and one long sob
which dissipates in all directions
and the wind carries it on
"Farewell, old country!"
"We won't forget you, old country!"
But suddenly the train sets off hurried on
by an order given in a non-Polish tongue
and head by head
body by body
the sign of the cross made in a sudden impulse
the last glistenings of a town to be forgotten
a Belorussian leaf sticks
to the compartment window
my mother holds the picture of the Virgin tight
my father watches over his Singer machine
in the rhythm of the wheels
in the rhythm of the tears
to the beat of a prayer
to the beat of disillusionment
on to the west!
as if we were being taking away to be shot
off into an uncertain future
from the land of the dispossessed

III.

I never said farewell to that town
I will never get to know my way around it
I constantly wake up on its streets
with scruffed knees with a box
of building blocks in my hands
I am woken by the singing of women on their way
from Sunday vespers
and the swearing of the men in the cherry
orchard drinking some illegally distilled brew

———

I stood still on the threshold searching for something
and all I can hear is the deaf rumbling of train wheels
That train travels on
it will never stop again

May 1984

Aleksander Jurewicz

Clouds over Lida

to my mother

Clouds over Lida, heavy
clouds, – as if made of lead or silence
Lost from sight just like the town
Nothing is left from our time here, there is
nothing – my memory struggles
down blind alleys, across washed out
photographs, into a ruined house . . .
(That once your youth was here
that I once ran around this place –)
It all disintegrates as if made of ash.
Between the walls a scream stops short
like silent sobbing immediately before real agony –
are those wild geese in their final flight
or has someone crushed a rowanberry.
So the town is no more, is not even
dreamt – just those clouds, my first
clouds

1986

Anna
Czekanowicz

Czekanowicz was born in Sopot in 1952, and studied at the Polish department of Gdańsk University. She was a member of the Wspólność group of poets in the late 1970s, and made her debut in 1976 with a set of poems entitled *Ktoś kogo nie ma* (Someone Who Isn't There, Gdańsk). Subsequent volumes of poetry include *Więzienie jest tylko we mnie* (The Prison is Merely Within Myself, Gdańsk 1978), *Pełni róż obłędu* (A Full House of the Roses of Madness. Gdańsk 1980), *Najszczersze kłamstwo* (The Sincerest Lie, Gdańsk 1984) and most recently *Śmierć w powietrzu* (Death in the Air, Gdańsk 1991).

My Prophecy

– I make the bed every day
  and tuck my children in
  People say that they are not children
  rather dreams that hold me tight

– I also walk down streets
  and listen carefully to
  the way trams grind along the tracks
  it's true I'm afraid of the noise

– I devote a great deal of time to myself
  then I think as I ought to
  Luckily I quickly forget
  and I start to bite my nails again

– I know it will be a few more days yet
  the sort that bring nothing
  I know I commit minor offences
  because other people do too
  I know how it will all end

Marina Tsvetaeva

I suppose I just wanted to believe
the Revolution had disposed of those closest to me
had taken away from me the vestiges of beauty
as well as the pathetic interest
in women's flowing dresses
I suppose I just wanted to believe
I had escaped merely to be able to come home again
the Revolution had given enormous strength to other poets
and I could not bear the barking
of émigré journalists
I suppose I just wanted to believe
There was no place in Europe
for such as me
subtle women poets
who earned their daily bread by night
I suppose I just wanted to believe in that
as I got off the train
I saw there was no one waiting for me

Saint

ecstacy is carnage
it is only the recently dead to the world
who are god's aviary
so tell me then you fine fisherman of the stammerers
(it's not a matter of moving the lips
these words simply remain unuttered)
why is ecstacy an abyss
rather than swinging beneath the heavens
and the final blow
a cracked bell with an exhausted heart
rings out with a sparseness
and taking a step backwards out of sheer dread
the body is covered with the sweat of anxiousness
unworthy of its triumph
he is embarassed by the violence of humility
a sacrifice has been offered
the fire of a holocaust trembles
and shoots straight up
enough . . .
with his fingers he explores prayer's outspread hair-suit

with the tip of his broken fingernail he giuseppe di copertino
wrote his epistle to god
yes the one by blaise cendrars
sowed letters of sand
between the tanned side of an animal's hide
and the air slowly rising upwards with him
so you do love me, lord?
you want to raise me up into your presence
but I am still far too heavy
turn away your eyes I fear I shall cry

behold father prior is threatening me
with his fist he points to the unpeeled potatoes
the unswept courtyard oh yes, I know
I am lazy and stupid oh so stupid
that my own mother could not love me

father can you see her the one who has tucked her skirt up
high
and having lifted her voluptuous behind up to god
she ties the sheaves with straw tell me please
is she praising the lord or do her generously
revealed thighs displease your eyes or perhaps just
like me you are experiencing a pleasant thrill

lord
I would so much like to be an ordinary man
to plough the fields have a home a mother and a woman
just like that one as faithful as a dog
animals in the yard and children

....

lord how generously you bear me in your arms

Time Pretending That it Passes

the last woman is never betrayed
the last dream remains untold
the last day is without end
and the last lover has nothing else to give
the last word is never a scream
while the last line remains unwritten
blood sinks into the ground

the picture opens and steps out of the frame
the body's slow oval announces dawn's entrance
luring from the gloom the contours of hated objects
that have collected in the corner of your room
and once more they inflame the pungent blood
of my lover

we are on the edge of an abyss
we balance on a silken thread
which we have strapped to our throat
under which there still pulsates a sliver
of my particularity never entirely shanghaied by sex

foliage is not green yet redness is rebellion
do not lose everything in bronze do not blur
the azure the murmering with colourlessness do not open my
eyes
do not unfold my hands do not let me fall asleep
do not leave do not shut down do not step back into the
frame

Anna Czekanowicz

Witch

slender pine black oak
dark cave by the quicksand
I cast my spell on you

where are the countless hordes
of cursed women not yet crammed into
the whole blackness of the world's
burnt pans scrubbed floors
stench of boiling underwear and the washing
menstrual blood and screaming childbirth
men the bull-kings lords of delight
that's where you will find me

where are all those women
who want a different lover every year
and who embitter themselves hex hex
who want to rule and fight
homeless wandering women
on the fine edge of day and night
with a glint in their eyes setting fire to the gloom
that's where I am

fragile glassy but
to you unbreakable
wounding the festering sores
with more new poisonous herbs

where do you build stakes of hatred
full of fire
where you want to chain me
where you want me to blaze
in the wind that will disperse my ash
and bear away my high-pitched scream
to give you that dark ecstacy

that's where I will always be

*   *   *

my fear wears a red dress
and he loves me to distraction
he never ever abandons me
he cannot bear other people
anybody whose words might upset
what is (in his view) our relationship

my fear interprets my dreams
distorts words said by others
likes to stroke my back
and often looks me straight in the eyes

my fear is the most faithful of mistresses
he claims he knows my past and future
he likes to walk down dark alleys
or along the night's misty bridges

my fear swears every evening
that he will never ever leave me

Anna Czekanowicz

Lady Macbeth of the Twentieth-Century

idiots
what did you expect
for thirty years
Jiang Qing
patiently bided her time
waited for the day when
she could include a billion photographs of herself
in a billion little red books
and the inscription Chairwoman of the Central Committee
thrown in the face of the Communist Party of China

sad grey-haired Jiang Qing
you don't know whether she's still alive do you
she is though – she's just not waiting any more
death will get her now anyway

so what if Jiang Qing
did not become a great star
of Chinese film musicals
the small girl from Shanghai waits for you every night
she did not gain ultimate power over you all
not even with her expressive gestures or supple figure
enveloped in the fragile mist of a negligé
she did not attain the heights of power through self-sacrifice
it was that ugly coarse pair of overalls
no style just identical day after day
and those terrible years at the side of
that narrow-minded Chinese with the limited imagination
how was it he managed to hold you all by the throat
how did he do it how did he succeed
perhaps we should have another try
there are still a couple of years left
one more *qeng feng*
another cultural revolution
eliminate those who oppose
there are still a couple of billion left anyway
water give me some water
bring me a bowl full of clean blood

A Poem For Today

to Juleczka, Miś and Maciek

installed on life's surface
of drawing room furniture during a summer holiday
in a false past
of which only the human masses survive
(revolutions parties coups wars
strikes concentration camps)
instead of that single person who had been alive
and then died a foreigner
alienated from everything
like a hook in an empty room

don't ever rely on other people
do not believe people
each one is like a played card
like all those sad days
which you must still live through
like the insults whispered behind your back
like your loneliness
and the knocking of the clock

you as much as anyone else have made trouble
whoever you might have been
not even the most appropriate
hero of your own night-time dreams
but given there is no other
you young man even if nondescript
must sit down and write
but that's not the end of it
you may still need to do infinite amounts
about time about which nothing yet has been said
although you suffer and are involved
and you don't know how to cope

do you know anything about those people
who live on despite what you write

when you say women children boys
do you know that there is no plural
but only endless singularities
tears kisses knives and murders
that every secret policeman is unique
even if he approaches you a thousand times

it is good to say out loud
it's alright
and nothing has happened again
does it help when wind blows into your eyes
and you know that you still have not got used to
this world which seems to be written down
even before anything has yet happened

everything is so natural
you have come through it all
like you live through a dream
and you did not stand still
you had demonstration in your blood
not teaching not speaking
and you decided at once
to magnify something insignificant
which only your passion
allows you to discern
so that it might stand there in front of everyone
that is how your own theatrical career began
a life so modest
yet it crept onstage
and then retreated deep inside
so deep
that suspicion was impossible

what you thought lost
reappears one day in its proper place
untouched delicate newer
as if someone had been looking after it all the time
and on top of your blankets there is the fear
that a crumb rolling off the bed

will fall glassily and shatter
and with this everything will crash
everything forever
the fear that the edge of an envelope
of a letter just torn open
is unbelievably valuable (god knows why)
and that in the whole room
there is not enough secure space
the fear that when you fall asleep
some number will begin to grow inside you
and that there will not be enough space for it
the fear that you may start to scream
and people will run up to your door
and then you might betray yourself
and tell everything that you are afraid of
and the fear that you may say nothing
since everything is unuttered

can you choose seclusion
in the same way as you choose
death out of terror
the slow palpitation of the heart
the pressure on the ear drums
and possession by your own musculature
can you
just not get up one morning
and shut yourself off
from all the lies of ordinary life
and the grandiose calls of those
who detest you

It won't be one of the informers of this world
but in fact your closest friend
who will be the first to strike you on the cheek
he will denounce you
accuse you behind your back
when you won't even be able to
say a word in your own defence
he will hide behind worthy slogans
and the symbolic cleanness of his hands

he will not even come up to you
when you are in tears
but he

one day you will fall in love with the darkness
when you walk down that gloomy alleyway
where you were constantly assaulted by fear
you can sense the night entering into you
and it does not hurt it is such delight
when you can see no one
yet you feel a thousand eyes upon you
memorising every single step you take
it is that day now
when you want to see no one
when you have nothing to say
you have not yet gone mad
you do not strip your skin down
but still the suspicion grows inside
you now know for sure
that you will never escape
and you will not suddenly
burst like a bubble

until finally on that day
when you stand in front of a closed window
and you will call all of those
who did not lose their nerve
and those who have died inside
you will curse reality
in all the colours of the rainbow
in all its manifold religions
words dreams politics and megaphones
tearing you to shreds in all the circumstances
which might get you locked away
drive you onto the street with the mob
stick a plaster over your mouth
wake you from your dreams

you haven't got a chance

Travel Poem

I'm talking to you – but it isn't
my fault if you can't hear me
J. Brodsky

there's no point in looking for life when travelling
there are only suitcases
unpacked then repacked
taken in and out again
planes trains and taxi cabs
outstretched palms
expecting a tip

there's no point in searching out new friends when travelling
there are only people
saying hello or goodbye
entering or leaving
faces backs or shoulders
words flung
backwards

there's no point in looking for a poem when travelling
there are only letters
delivered and posted
set to one side unread
a black sky unstarlit
the stomach painfully contracting
the red star of *au revoirs*

Anna Czekanowicz

Iowa Iowa Iowa

it really is rather strange
but the world is full of living people

iowa avenue in iowa, iowa
is such a strange street
it starts at the old town hall
and then about half a mile along
there's a fork
on the right there are some dime stores
k-mart and sycamore mall
and vast numbers of small white houses
on the left there are just houses
at one of the intersections
a really cheap bookstore
I like to go there
and read the books
why don't I buy one
they're really cheap
the salesman is surprised
and then I have to explain
that I don't have a home here
that I'm just walking around
I'm not even really sure where I'm going
that there are no mice or ants
on the lawns beside the white houses
only cockroaches are everywhere
and I'm getting to like them more and more
because day by day
I'm targetting my shoe better
even at these most humble examples
of american living standards
I suppose I'll be wasting this particular talent
back in gdańsk

Bronisław Maj

Studied Polish at the University of Kraków where he now teaches. From 1977-81 Maj worked as a scriptwriter and actor in the KTO Theatre, and was subsequently in charge of the arts section of the local bi-weekly *Student* which was suspended because of Martial Law. From 1983 he (with Jerzy Pilch) organised the spoken journal *Na Głos* (Out Loud), a magazine format based on three hours of readings, lectures, poetry, prose, interviews, etc., regarded as one of the most important independent fora in mid–1980s Poland. *Na Głos* has since 1989 become one of the most important quarterly publications in Poland. Maj is now its editor. Maj's reputation rests on his poetry collections: *Wiersze* (Poems, 1980), *Taka wolność* (That Sort of Freedom, 1981), *Wspólne powietrze* (The Air We Breathe, 1981), *Zmęczenie,* Fatuigue, 1986), and an émigré collection of his poems entitled *Zagłada świętego miasta* (The Annihilation of the Holy City, London 1986). In addition to writing poetry, Maj is also a literary critic, essayist and scriptwriter for the cinema.

*   *   *

An August afternoon. Even from this far away I can hear
the noise of the sparkling River Raba. We look up at the
                                        mountains together
my mother and I. How pure the air is:
every single black spruce on Mount Lubon can be seen
as clearly as if it were growing in our own back garden.
An astonishing phenomenon – one that surprises both
                                        mother
and myself. – I am four years old and I do not know
what being four years old means. I am
happy: I do not even know the meaning
of being or happiness. I do know that mother can feel
and see the same as I do. And I know,
know for certain that today
as every evening we will take a long
walk to the woods.
Soon.

*   *   *

I shall never write a long poem: everything
that I have encountered here deters me
from telling lies: it exists in between
two mouthfuls of air, in a single
glance, in a single seizure of the heart. And I am
only now, and what is here with me
is only enough for a dozen or so
short lines of verse, a poem as brief as the life-span
of a cabbage butterfly, of the glint of light on the crest of a
                                                        wave,
of a human being, or of a cathedral. A dozen or so lines
                                                        then,
and what exists between them: the everlasting
glistening of light, the eternity of a butterfly's life,
and humankind transcending
death.

*　　*　　*

Objects captured in still life: they give no sign
of living: indeed display no signs at all. This
floorboard creaks beneath my shoe,
because the wood is warped, and that is the only
reason. It creaks. It is not – moaning,
not – warning me. That mania for seeing in objects
the image and likeness of other things, the determined
                                                    search
for proofs of indispensible relevance, the need for
reassurance regarding the permanent discomfort of being
in this place. Objects require no scaffolding. They just are –
confidently and effortlessly. Stones do not
sustain themselves by means of the worn-out imagery of
the heart. Yet lonely and lost, we forever injure
ourselves on their cold edges, gashing ourselves
on their needles and jags: so there can
at least
at the very least be this fraternalisation
of blood.

*   *   *

It was all rather different to the way they later said it was.
It's true you found it hard to live, but then you didn't know
                                                        how
to die: your despair and enthusiasm, hope and pain
were not different from anyone else's. Death came
later. They started it at first, and now they are watching
you – from over there. As if you had never been alive.
                                                Never:
a warm light from the West on the town spires, the smooth
fur of a dog called Mescal beneath your hand, the smell
of fires, the cries of a bird that arouse vague feelings, her
name, uttered so softly, hunger pangs, the pleasure of a job
well done – you never had those things, so they say. Death –
                                                        that
much is certain – they can only perceive you through
                                certainties – in the light which
glared into your eyes, there forever remains your gaze, an
animal's fur is smoother than if
you had not touched it, she would have been a different
                                                woman if
you had not loved her. Nothing ever ends. Death has
just moved on. It is all here. It is just different to the way
                                                they say
it was.

*   *   *

This strange evening: I am sitting in the garden, pine trees
still clearly outlined against the sky, nearby
mothers call to their children to come in, a train clatters
passing away into the distance, a soft clatter. I think about
                                                    my life
as if it were already a closed and completed thing.
I do not want to return to anything. Nor change
or correct anything, I am pure. The blurred border between
me and this evening: with my whole body I can feel
stars rustle, pines creak, wheels
softly clatter. Pure, but expecting the new birth and
                                                    beginning
of – what? Will there be trees there, or the approaching
clatterings – will these rekindle the vague and pleasant
memory of this evening, will there be
children and mothers, will one of them call me in from
the place I am sitting, and will there
definitely be pine trees? – I am unable to
transcend what I have come to
know here, to desire anything other than
happiness.

* * *

Everything that this moment
really was – has remained
within it. It exists in no other
now: evening and a road leading to a station,
a cloud of crows above the parkland, a handshake
and a train that only set off after all this.
Not much really, not much at all. It will be enough
many years later in a cold empty room
to bite your clenched fist between your teeth. –
Don't scream now: just hold this pose long enough, with
                                        bravura.
Describe: the evening, the road, the cloud of crows and the
                                        train, everything
that was there. The rest does not exist. It
is just a memory. Only my
memory, me, indescribable.

*   *   *

Night in the mountains, a storm. A shelter full of people.
                                              Lightning and
– as ephemeral as a leaf – an interval holding out for
the thunderclap: how can it be measured, that span of a few
                                    seconds? what is
a second? – an epoch in the civilization of a raindrop, the
                                        entire life of
a microbe, the time taken for two or three human breaths,
                                    possibly even four
when rushed – in fear, pain, love. A couple of seconds
in which birth and death, or indeed nothing, insert
                                  themselves – how
can these be measured? – I could deliberate no more
before the thunderclap collapsed crashing over the
                                      mountains.
Seated around the fire, the people sighed with relief.
But there will be a repeat performance: the exhausting lapse
                                    between
the flash and the clap, time for a few thoughts at most, or an
                                    entire
life: there is hardly enough time to think, to register the
                                  human faces,
their unsettled expressions, hands gripped tightly, breath
                                  held in,
looking at them, you can barely manage to understand our
                                  ephemeral
age: there are no lightning flashes, and no echoing thunder
claps, just this extended interval –
the final leaf
of time.

*   *   *

Mine is a particular imagination: it sees
a tear, the odd-shaped leaf on the crest of a maple
tree, the wrinkle on a face I had fallen in love with
when young and pure. It is also banal:
willing to grant as the essence of things the scene
I now observe, a chance
encounter along a deserted path between a young boy
and a squirrel, which warily
approaches his imploringly outstretched hand.
Driven by hunger it is unaware of the light
which – kindled at this precise instant – will never
be extinguished in the mature man. My imagination
does not even reach the limits of what is possible:
it is not terrified by the yellow (or purple)
flare with which the sun is spotted, or by a sudden draught of
damp dust, or by that insistent pain
beneath the skull that puts an end to all of this.
It sees this as nothing. Nothing instead of.
Instead of the face that I love. Instead of a maple tree.
                                                        Nothing
instead of the essence of a thing consummated
in the communion between man and beast. Nothing
of the essence of a thing. Nothing –
beyond imagination.

*   *   *

Who will bear witness to these times?
Who will record it all? not one of us, certainly:
We have lived here too long, have breathed in this age too
                                                    deeply,
are too loyal to it to be able to tell the whole truth about it.
Or even to tell the truth at all. In loyalty
I say 'justice' while contemplating the dark joy of revenge,
I say 'dignity', but want to impose my own will
I say 'concern' but think 'us' and 'them',
and – 'what they did to me'. I have nothing else
to say in my defence: just loyalty. And weakness:
that I hated evil, that I lied in order to defend
the truth, while contempt was my diseased pride.
Hatred, contempt and lying: all this for so many years
all in order to survive and stay pure. But it can't be done:
survive and stay pure. At best you can survive.
Remaining – dumb. So the question: who will bear witness?
is asked knowing it won't be one of us, or anybody
else. So not a word more. An empty age.
More than any other, crammed with life, because
it is our life, and there will not be another. This turmoil,
the shouting, crying, laughing and weeping – is our common
anthem, without words, not even a single word
that would ever speak up
for us.

*   *   *

Beyond the window there is rain, a glass of tea on the table,
a lamp: That's how, perhaps naively, I can see you
in five, twenty or one hundred and twenty-five
years, reading this poem: thinking about me, a man
of twenty, or one hundred and twenty years earlier – and
                                                    how
I lived. My age and I: hopelessly tired people,
some dates, places of failure, some names: the curses that we
                                                    repeated
then with the childish hope of living, more foolish than you
in wisdom, which time will have given you, the one alive
                                                    after all this
after us, after everyone. There is so little
I have to tell you, as much as anyone else. But after all
I was alive and I don't want to die completely: but remain
everyman to you, the subject of statistical
compassion or contempt. What has only been
only me, is beyond history. So I will speak about myself
in the only language available to both of us: about the smell
                                                    of moist
urban dust beyond the window pane (rain has fallen), about
                                                    the table
rubbing against my elbows, the ticking of a clock, the taste
                                                    of hot
tea, about the light of the lamp that hurt my eyes
as I was writing this poem – in the universal language of all
five immortal
senses.

*   *   *

In the heavy air of this unsettled summer, through the
                                          commotion
of the oppressive town, she walks along: in a loose skirt, a
                                          lightly-coloured blouse,
like the ones worn by so many girls this summer – what
                                          makes her so
distinct? – she looks without registering us and our gaze
                                          cannot touch
her either: her proud white forehead, held high,
her calm and confident movements, unavailable, different: a
                                          trickle
of cool rain in this crowded, clammy street, she is
                                          immaculately
pure. But in the city someone
knows her tears and exhaustion well
and her proud, white
breasts when bared . . .

70

*   *   *

At first you did not grasp the meaning of what you saw: one
                                                    evening
after long hours on a beach, you by yourself – deep in
                                                    thought:
not missing even a second of the royal splendour of those
                                        final moments
of the sun: the shimmering of fiery and pearly waves, the
                                        clouds' dancing
icebergs and that powerful inexhaustible rumbling – within
                                the never-ending miracle
of a sunset – finally enlightened, you understood . . . Then
                                you walked back
from there: through the warm gloom of a pine forest –
                                        sudden silence
and darkness, a sandy path and then a road, and the open
                                light – that's when you
saw this scene: in front of a small cabin, on a bench, an old
man (he could have been your father) swaying, tapping his
                                                    feet –
he was playing a rather simple tune on his accordeon – in
                                        front of him
a young boy (he could have been your son) danced and
                                                    jumped
wearing a baseball cap, singing awkwardly. Up to that point
                                                    nothing
connected these disparate things: first the opulence of the
                                elemental and then humble
human pleasures, except that: you saw them immediately
                                        one after the other
and only you could be their correspondent: to be in between
grandfather and grandson, to take your place among the
                                        unknown names
of father and son, you. – That much you realised then. And
                                        not until today,
illuminated, do you see them both again, and hear an
                                        extraordinary song

71

from humble royal lips – so now you know: this is how a
                                     jealous God frowns upon
you: he demands to be recognized in his quietest
creatures – like you: in living
faces made in the exact image
and likeness.

*   *   *

Childhood's impoverished landscapes: a few simple
                                        locations, certainly
not the most impressive sort: the sleepy summer retreat just
                                        outside Łódź, Gorce,
the lime outcrops with a view out on to Jasna Góra. There
                                        was no choice. And no
refusing: when you think, or even dream, of those hills – you
                                        see nothing
else: Mount Luboń's tranquil wooded ridges and its black
                                        outline; dozing
under the alders, the Grabia will always remain The River,
                                        and the sun
on Częstochowa's dark towers will be the only illumination
                                        you have
been granted: your time has run its course – you are here
now. Cut off from the worlds miraculous revelations,
                                        imprisoned in
what you were: condemned. But still you are here: go up to
                                        the window
spread your arms wide, look further, harder: release it, but
                                        resist
its transience. Yes, the world's. You can grant it a reprieve
                                        by saturating it:
in every river it dozes there , one green drop from the rain
                                        off the alders, and it
is precisely from the mountain where the monastery stands
                                        that
the light, as it spills down, will indefatigably
reclaim the darkness and there establish the brilliant
white towers of the Eternal
Cities.

*   *   *

No one has claimed it: homeless
and untouched. Not even a hint of despair or regret: That
                                        agonizing
sense of shame, fear that it must not be repeated – that
is all that remains. To be forgotten and cancelled: a
                                        transitory
age is what those will say who manage to speak of
a single human life so easily. Destroy the evidence. Even
the most threatening, since it is unintended and pure: a
                                        couple, their child
asleep, stares for one last time at a small
photograph: a fair-haired woman, and a man, both very
                                        young, embracing
on a honey-yellow July afternoon thick with insects and the
                                        smell of grass
staring at the camera lens thirsty and curious, from the porch
of an old house among the reddish pines. That house, the
                                        pine trees –
stand there to this day confirming – thats how it was. So all
                                        the faster
in sheer panic they obliterate her, my our faces from
the photograph, believing that as a result of this
the worst cannot happen, though it
exists.

74

Jan
Polkowski

Born in Kraków in 1953, Polkowski studied Polish literature at the
University there, and between 1977 and 1979 became an active
member of the student Solidarity committee, as well as the editor
of the clandestine *samizdat* publishing group *kos* (the Kraków
Student Publications). In the Solidarity period he founded the
independent publishing group ABC, but was interned as a dan-
gerous element on 13 December 1981. He continued, after the
amnesty to work in the underground as editor of *Arka* (the Ark),
and since 1989 the whole enterprise has gone legal, and has been
expanding. Polkowski is also the editor in chief of the conservative
nationalist daily Czas (Time) published in Kraków. His first poems
were published in the underground quarterly *Zapis* in 1978, and
his subsequent volumes appeared only on *samizdat* presses. *To nie
jest poezja* (That's not poetry – NOWa 1980); *Oddychaj głęboko*
(Breathe in Deeply – ABC 1981); *Ogień. Z notatek 1982-83* (Fire.
From My Notebooks, 1982-83 – Półka Poetów 1983) and *Drzewa*
(Trees – Oficyna Literacka 1987). An émigré edition of his poems
was published in London as *Wiersze* (Poems – Puls 1986). His first
selected anthology *Elegie z tymowskich gór i inne wiersze* (Elegies
from the Tymowo Hills and Other Poems) was published in
Kraków by the eminent Catholic publishing house Znak in 1990.

Eternity's Flow

The language of things, the poetry of pure objects
without a shadow of desire when uttering the word 'table'
to say anything more.
But to say it so
transparently that it is possible to see
before us that unique, warm, slightly wobbly table,
weighed down with odours, fingered childishly by
the deceased, with its one drawer
contained between these table legs that pull out,
so that you can see
what happens in poetry
the original rotational force of this earth.

*   *   *

The soothing valleys have come to rest in this poet.
The sun of freedom, Susette, Hellas – home of the
                                        tyrannicides
is ever more distant. Though he, Hölderlin, in rags
and without food, when waking or sleeping
forever longs for it
in the German language. For that is the language used by
this poet from the Neckar's banks.

To see God with mine own eyes, he wrote
and I believe the poet was granted the grace of seeing Him,
for who else could he really have implored
Pray let me always
last in this truth.

A Flag Fluttering in the Wind

Poetry will never come back,
it will not be released from your tortured
verse,

from your body discarded in the snow,
from the Lvov prison cell,
from the Lubianka headquarters, Moscow.

Like a young, diaphanous girl
descended into the bowels of the earth
beyond the Berlin Wall
of Europe and Death

(unaware that someone is taking notes
softly she repeats:
> *You don't really need this poetry*
> *avoid all contact with metaphors*).

Jan Polkowski

The Envoy of Mr. X

You have not survived to bear witness,
which like the smoke from a discarded victim
refuses to disperse from the burning cities

Your body – that is the beginning and the end of time
so do not let it become the injured archive
for some poems or the fairy-tales of dreamers
and fools

You did not survive it all to testify
against it: the world is too close a relative
of your children

All roads lead
circuitously to the place where you lie down
to take the sleep of the just

History has its laws, this is why you should watch
from the perspective of civilisation without exaltations,
how a small nation is dying
how its last generations are suffocating

But do not lose hope
perhaps you will not wake up on the far side of the prison's
narrow gate, with an irregular two pointed star
sewn into your flesh,
perhaps you will not see that moment, perhaps you will die
before your birth into the people chosen
for annihilation

Before they find you outside the city limits in the uniform
of a worker or a philosophy student
with a face covered by that liberal Communist rag 'Polityka'
describing the Fascist practices
of South American police forces

79

Young Poets of New Poland

Before you understand the insult: Jew-boy!
or: Polack!

Go, remain faithful
to the flag made of black and white barbed wire
and to the generals
of your daily prayer

*   *   *

I have said it all. Yes
I have.
And now I feel empty and uncleansed
like a square after a demonstration.
(Didn't I understand anything?)
I went in and listened to my son whimpering
and that was the Word of God, a zither, a vale of plenty.
I felt like a fisherman, who though hungry
sets free his catch, and returns home with pride.
It was quiet, I carried you
in my stride
but at my back there stirred
an all-devouring fire.

October 1981

* * *

Do not write anything. Let others speak,
and even if they never used words like:
revolution, freedom, dignity, humiliation,
even if their tongues were only flesh
and not zithers, frescoes or swords, allow
them to speak. Let the blood run
and the fire spread, let the trunk of the lime-tree thicken
let the water and the fruit wander.
Do not hold back your heart,
let it drink and listen.

*   *   *

You wanted to say too much, you dull words
How ridiculous your conceited hope is that grammar can be
                                                a match for death.

But even if I was your hostage
No one cares whether I prove myself faithful, or
                                                compromised.

But here I am, alive, and the unsettled surface of the fruits
                                                of paradise
Pulsates beneath my finger.
I and my supporters: the black water, the fragile grass, the
                                                sweet wind
We distance ourselves in order to reach the source *en masse*,
from whose letters mere ants cannot drink.

How futile your paper curses are, closely observed
by the breath and fire that
the white rainbow of words does not encompass.

"Things Unuttered Tend to Non-existence"
(Czesław Miłosz)

You took pleasure in life, poets, all the while forgetting you
must create the world out of sensitivity and pain.
It seemed to you that wives, children, relatives, your own
land,
permanent appointments could be excuses for the barrenness
of your hands.
But in the end has anyone really divided the darkness of
objects
from the luminosity of words?
Has there been anyone impervious to the seductive image of
the kingdom,
who was willing to choose the everlasting existence of a
radiant couplet?

(Speak book)
At the end of a rambling day there is another poem:
bread, cheese, water, woman,
And so it is done.
(The sun paled and entered into the seas
disconnected from the land.)

Jan Polkowski

It is Good . . .

It is good that things occur, that cannot ever last:
a lime tree straining to the last moment to blossom,
a house wishing to continue the male line of the family,
a city determined to maintain at least its foundations beneath
                                                    the grass.

It is good if there is a fertile root to a country
from which, in a gentler climate, the branches of all the arts
                                                    can grow.

It is good to feel beneath the ocean's fingertips the sweet and
                                                    unending
texture of a Ukrainian lullaby intoned by a nanny already
                                        assumed into heaven.

It is good, too, if the seven armed fire blazes with dancing
                                        Jewish smocks,
the incantation of an Orthodox priest sounds, and a sober
                                    German prayer is uttered.

It is good to preserve the graves of eccentric contemporaries,
                                                to honour them
on the rippling altars of the air.

It is good to rely on metaphors instead of biographies as a
                                        home for the senses
in search of words' frontiers in the language of childhood.

And finally it is good to feel below this sheet of paper a
                                                    table,
which could have carried the face of God in a boarded-up
                                        Slovak church,

it could have taken the form of mountain pastures caught in
                                                    a trap,
it could have had the expression of the priest who saved
                                                    Christ,

it could have been hammered together from denunciations,
                                                   betrayals,
or the countenance of Marx's singed portraits,
with that nobility so deserving of compassion,
this table could have been left behind by German, Jews or
                                                          Poles
– but it is simply made of wood.

*   *   *

Does the moment of birth demand depicting that crucial gap
                                    of memory?
The eternity of evolving? That moment of first sunlight?
                                    When She,
The Woman Reading a Letter or *The Weigher of Pearls* stood
                                    in concentration,
withdrew into herself in order to form me?

Thank you Vermeer of Delft, my foster brother,
it was You who assured that my Mother in her Dutch cap
and a yellow kaftan, in the pearly light of the wrought-iron
                                    window
confidently expected child-birth.

I, then, was the ark in the ambers of Her waters,
the dove and pigeon, the male and female principles of the
                                    innocent world.
I had wanted to convey within me more than is given to
                                    others to do,
and particularly the manner in which the world, one
                                    fragment after another,
was able to simulate Your paintings.

But what work of human hand can shed light upon itself?
So my chance of understanding myself were faint.
Listening to this tale of my own genesis, remember
that I also longed to be delivered.

Thus it was, then, in the small body folded into the womb's
                                    sail
that the synthesis was completed: I watched the fugue grow,
I heard the ochre and the white, I touched the haze of
                                    words.

And You carried me light-footed across an arid ocean
holding me within Yourself until the resurrection.

Urszula Benka

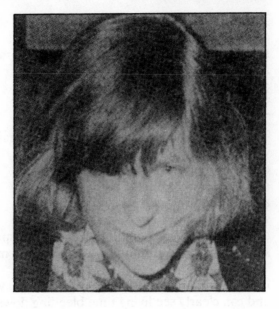

Born in Wrocław in 1955, where she studied psychology and Polish at the city's university, Benka made her debut in 1975 in the local monthly cultural revue *Odra* in 1975, and her poems were then published in various magazines and newspapers. Her published volumes include *Chronomea* (Kraków, 1977), *Dziwna rozkosz* (Strange Ecstacy, Wrocław 1978), *Nic* (Nothing, Kraków 1984), *Perwersyjne dziewczynki* (Perverse Little Girls, Warsaw 1984) and most recently *Ta mała tabu* (That Little Taboo, Warsaw 1991) For the volume *Chronomea,* Benka won the Stanisław Grochowiak Poetry Prize. Having left Poland for Paris in the early eighties, Benka now lives in New York, but continues to publish in Poland.

A Convent of Schizophrenic Nuns

Let's burn this witch
– then we'll be warmer

Try to understand – we have been accused of madness
and also of a certain underhand sort of sin:
namely that time has become the ultimate insult to us
and a dizzying mirror
all this is the state of utter anxiety

Try to understand –
The convents prostrate in the afternoon heat
where each glance liberates drops
of nervous music from the flowers
and where vows of hand extension
are continually being renewed
so both zeal and whiteness
as well as all despised suffering can be grasped –
such convents have something of a choked magic about
                                                                them:
in them you are a hundred years old and have yellow fingers
and can clearly see living time bleeding down the walls
flowing right up to the altar – like the hair of God
and these are not hallucinations
but our compulsions:
withdrawal

We all withdraw – under our closed eyelids
where we have erected a cemetery
we lay clocks on a stretcher in their agony
and embalm them together with their silence
and then the immortalised silence begins to accumulate
we are the extension of the silence too
locked in our tomb we die
with exact precision like terrified clocks
nevertheless sensitively reproducing time
an unbounded point of ambush.

Urszula Benka

We are frightened. For these are sorts of fairy-tale pictures
which we can only wound, like any measured metallic

motion
and that is our understanding of time:
it needs to be killed
perhaps within ourselves.

They accuse us of madness – but can there be any better way
of going into hiding
than to become the mechanism itself
and so really not have anything to do with what creates us
or with what we are bound to measure

We murder bloodstained infinity
the world's blind catastrophe – just by looking it
straight in the eye
and not giving way to its sightless stare

Suddenly we know that we are so very dead
so ceaselessly dead
that we simply get bored by our own demise
it is this boredom that is the origin of time

April 1975

The Four Horsemen of Human Passion

All I desire today is pain, a conclusion, evil days
in expectation of this I walk out into the road.
Its stone ribbon solidifies in its bends and curves –
someone will say that Satan in the form of a snake
has turned into stone inside it and heaven
examines its complexion in the devil as if in a mirror
while the shadows of the clouds
hold the beast radiating sparks
down on the pavement
will say that love, hate and fear –
the three elements of the beast like the beast's three quarter
                                                    phases –
will cast down into the depths
their dust-ridden cores
The fourth element
will gather the husks –
And on that road at dawn I saw a woman
with a stove-sized sack to contain the seed. She said that she
                                                    wanted
the road's cobblestones
to be unpassable and as proud as Babel,
so that on the bends and turnings of the way the hunchbacks
off-loaded their experiences
into her sack –
she wanted to bear the chalice
of the confusion of scripts,
and to satisfy the thirst of the road's grey mass with that
                                                    madness,
over its cobblestones Fear
turns as if it were a quern
and yet love and hate watch hard into the stone's madness
like two mirrors glaring into each others' eyes.
The arteries of the beaten path stand out
the grain separates from its husks
and I hear an old woman laughing,
that the Fourth element is drawing close
that the beast
rises today

in his last quarter
after the next bend –

The moon like a blue snake
renews its waxing journey on high
The day is ended.
She is ready, holding out her sack.

22.11.81 Grudziądz

Joy

An essentially strange pathology arose out of our love.
Passion only exasperates a narcissistic childhood
(a mutual narcissism, it is free of the alienation or the silence
                                        beside the spring . . .)
and only in that sense
do you remark on my nakedness – with one eyebrow raised –
you consider it with the expression of an aphorist
and your caress resembles
an aphorism
as we walk down cold, uninviting Avenue Duquesne.
But I submit quietly to these facts
with a matching, raised eyebrow,
I am never able to be as patient and brimming with charm
as when I wait for the climax
which can lash me or you
like a conductor's baton – with the unexpectedness of Strauss
in the shadow of a ball that unreels
the streets behind us . . .
the North blows down from the Champs Elysees
my childhood blossoms in my décolleté, and in your hand,
placed on my heart.

But our audience discreetly dozes
hugged by the violets in the conductor's buttonhole

2.12.83 Paris

Pedestal

The city was razed by fire in successive stages, whose levels
arranged themselves pyramidically in the form of a pedestal,
standing for the proof of the existence of things impossible.
Yet the City
was possible, and so too burning it down had become equally
possible
so utterly that no one under any conceivable circumstances
would be able to reconstruct it or even initiate an attempt
irrespective of failure or success
of renovating it.
All personal, practical and theoretical powers were burnt
down
and so too were methods, forms, questions, answers and
rationalisations,
even the Ultimate justification and consequence of such
conflagration,
and the stakes were burnt down as well.
The burnt City's irreducible existence endures in the perfect
sphere of the Pedestal
which in its essence is not complex but homogeneous,
unequivocal and impossible and thus
cannot be burnt down.

Well with Demon

The demon of our wedding has taken up residence
in a tin bucket by the well on the edge of the woods
and since he came we go there
separately
night after night:
I send down the bucket, you pull up the rope
and when we drink, with every mouthful our hands
move further away
and no voice
disturbs the clear splash
when the demon of our wedding takes his seat on the surface
of the water
as the bottom becomes visible he bares himself
and gives each of us an enormous umbrella:
beneath yours is our day,
beneath mine is our night,
so you have no night, and I have no day
and we return home seeing nothing through the umbrella's
canvas
and first we circle around the well, where
with those hands of his
which we do not know how to touch,
he bangs loudly against the sides of the tin bucket.

And then, deafened beneath the umbrellas
we smile sleepily and run all the way home
even though we did not know each other before
to make each other's violent acquaintance.

Urszula Benka

Dream Me

your dream petrifies in my soul
in a sort of underground cloister – down its tight corridors
following the breaches in your dreams I encounter the dead:
decomposing silk, like the modest schizophrenia of the
bracelets
is transformed on a song-book discarded during childhood
endless smiles
from fourteen-year old Phe
she is the shadow of your dream because other than the real
existence of rocks
besides the real fact of catacombs and of my scream with no
echo
in the deafening world of symbols
(I sometimes feel suffocated by such self-knowledge)
Phe is your flute
You sit at the entrance of a pot-hole, it is midday
the sea is silent at your back
a dog licks a watch wilting in the heat
the dog's saliva mingles with the shimmerings of the passing
hours
and dog is grey-haired and sea is grey-haired
and your playing enters into the glinting of the clock-face
like a glance
Sometimes Phe understands it and appears from
underground
like a shadow of the childood we spent together
gold in her hands is grey, a dusty pain
yellowed with the demands made by metaphors

when Phe's head rises up and is close to its full phase
the dog raises its head, howls quietly, and the watch on your
wrist loses its breath
You put the flute down
you only utter my name

evil's sadness in the underground lake splashes noiselessly
I float on my back naked in this tristesse – a dark wave
carries me like a piece of bark scribbled with words

I do not remember what route we take (all dimensions are
                                              adjacent here)
and so I take my place on the surface of the mirror
I see you I fall to my knees as if before the Resurrected One
and yet only the tears of your malleable watch
of your childhood have brought me the touch
of your hands

and the dog listens to you and the desert becomes weightless
                                              and hopeless
and the flute turns transparent;
Phe outlined like the moon's new phase illuminates your
                                              whisper:
dream of me
I shall lead you out of here more lovingly than Orpheus

Urszula Benka

Adam Hertz the Builder

I have constructed thirty seven mechanical angels
so far
and given them names and swords,
and each of the swords I have also named:
the first was called Egomunda, and the last
was called Esmeralda
(and indeed I honed it out of an emerald
as large as an obelisk)

My angels have no faith in me, and
when I pass by the cages designated for my swords
they state that I do not exist
and following a battle in their own blood they write out
                                                    proofs
of my non-existence,
which I believe firmly.

It is possible to believe anything, and I will it so to be
and the whole of my artistry
I dedicate to the raising
of a translucent temple where I shall duly honour
my swords, which astonish me so much
(and particularly Egomunda and Esmeralda
whose statues of mechanical metaphors
remain the ultimate mark of approval.
for my work)

Mystery depends on creating ever newer
Codices complete with their exegeses and apologetics
and these conflicts between
angels and swords, which just like banners
raise high my emblems
ambiguously etched on dark blue silk
containing within them
the anxieties of astronomy and theology.
And the angels like the sharp blades of the swords
engage in lengthy disputations and raise enormous armies,

and carry out covert assassinations
bringing with them the tortures of an insatiable audience.

My life, in as far as it exists at all, is subordinated
to these Codices. And in the end I feel the grace of
my swords flowing down onto me:
To those fallen for the truth of my non-existence
I shall build mausolea
of poetry and prophecy.

And my exertion is not isolated: I repeat
the deeds and the beliefs
of my master
Johann Ezechiel Krantz
whom on his deathbed angels and swords
judged and carried out
the sentence of execution,
which was just. And neither does my breast
tremble at the judgement of the swords.
And my disciple Johan Hertz will also construct
ever newer, ever more perfect
Codices, their Systems and their Mechanics,
and he will not tremble either.

Auto-da-fé

A girl is seated by a fire. It is night. Marshes – like madness
in the eyes of a soothsayer – gently sparkle among the alder
                                                          trees
an oak tree bears its shaggy brow of a giant
high above the forest,
and in the fire at the foot of the oak the bones turn
                                              relentlessly
the smoke defines pale bluish forms in the darkness;
a man, who is creeping up from behind to push her suddenly
into the flames – steals towards her from the reed beds.
There is only the wind. A boat dances nervously by the
                                                shoreline.
In the boat – a devil. Like a huge bird of prey on its nest,
or Charon the boatman– he watches his fellow conspirator
and from this hidden vantage point, through the movement
                                        of slippery branches
he sends the man his devilish dream.

The man dreams of a whole retinue of maidens rising from
                                                the ashes
who went before the girl unwarily
guarding the fire.
Young maidens' shadows graze the eyelids
of this keeper of the flame.
She senses nothing. She has lost all memory,
having entered into the logic of these rituals
not noticing the difference
between herself and the skeleton of the fire
which in a strong, bony retinue
circles the oak tree
looks into the marsh as if into a well
and its flames chase purplish hoops
high up into the sky beyond.
The girl sits motionless by the fire
totally at one with its inner order
and the man hidden among the reeds
that invisible huntsman

sent into this country from the opposite shore
manipulated mechanically by the devil's dreaming
senses his own hopelessness
when, carrying within him a devilish passion
he can not recognise what will be her stake
or what burns upon it:
bones,
memory
or is it consciousness.

Urszula Benka

Temptation

You should stop walking behind me like this –
I don't know these streets myself, clocks burn at the road's
turnings
it looks extraordinary
in rain that flashes so intensely with neon
I'm only going to spend under an hour in solitude
I want to shake hands with that hour on some helpless
square
yesterday for example I saw
a small boy casually stroking one
of those clocks alternately burn dark blue then emerald
green
and at the Pére Lachaise Cemetery
he exposed his closed eyelids to the rain
and it is only when I understand that child
that your smile penetrates me
so I want to see what he must have seen

The Last Stop Café

A nothing to write home about sort of establishment . . . on
Terribly Square, I Want You
and in the midst of all this there is fog, mad mirrors, the
stairway's keyboard.
Hawthorne's shadow serves coffee and punch.
only the stars above us are real but the night
is beginning to flow out of us
the shadows of our hearts twitch slightly in the coffee
grounds
the pact with the devil is reflected in the saddened greenish
eyes of my cat, Taboo –
inside them hieroglyphics glare like meteors, you and
Hawthorne . . .
the deepest shade of love . . .

And the water, sir, thinks intensely about us in the fountain
and in the night becomes an apostrophe of darkness
Taboo's tracks beneath the gas lamp fall silent and the stars
enchant
and grow up from the very roots of the Cosmos
On Terribly Square, I Want You Too – a nothing to write
home about
sort of establishment.
Except the climate here has such an English accent.
Isn't it a bit cold sitting here drinking
and watching Taboo's fur glisten when we stroke it?

Tadeusz Żukowski

Żukowski was born in 1955 in Gwardziejsk near Kaliningrad (CIS), formerly Koenigsberg, his parents refugees from the Novogrod area, now in Belorussia. Eventually the Polish-speaking family settled in Trzebiatów on the Polish Pomeranian coast. At first Żukowski went to school in Szczecin, where his first poems were written and published (1973), but his calling as a poet began with his studies in Polish at the University of Poznań. He has so far produced volumes of poems: *Ucho van Gogha* (Van Gogh's Ear, Wrocław 1982), *Wiersze najbielsze* (The Whitest of Poems, Poznań 1986), and *Księga listów* (A Book of Letters, Szczecin 1988). His current work in progress is a cycle entitled 'The Books of Dying and Birth'.

A Letter – Examination of Conscience

It is also an examination of the conscience. (Poetry). And
imagination –
Is a conversation with witnesses. With memory, which like a
net after a storm
Gets tangled in a mess of bream and roach, the lifeless
follicles of seaweed,
The drowned carcasses of seabirds and the warm coat of a
body lost
At sea. With the voices of those abandoned, unwelcomed,
and, all too often,
self-conscious: Why, on that hot close night, did you get up,
Get dressed and drown that homeless mongrel howling for
hours
Underneath the window... (mother's migraine?). Afterwards
it whined
Endlessly in your dreams. A crime remains a crime; even
when
The world is ending. You will never repay the debt of life to
an ant or a starling
(That damned rifle and the whispers of moronic sergeants),
or the priceless ball
Rolled by a hedgehog – not for the rest of the eternity
prepared for you by
God. If you have died with them – then you will be
resurrected with them too.
Will evil's defenceless victims then perhaps begin to love us
in return?

23.8.94, Poznań

Tadeusz Żukowski

A Letter Written in a Fever

O provincial life, damnation to me and death to us all!
How nagging are your by-ways, as anyone can savour
who changes the anguish of side-streets into bodies.
The River Rega runs scarlet then like an aorta; our home –
Mother, Czesław (my brother) and my sister are only its

atria

And valves, that's all – you cannot transplant the heart
In the same way that father regrafts a sweet-pea's shoot . . .

The clay clods

On which Leśmian (the poet) walked, grow here too under

boys'

Bare feet. The wind melts into the woods and the ribcage
Folds closed inclining an interior landscape. On the exterior:
A flushed body. The wide sea beside it is happiness.
You dive in, and, out of the blue, you are inside the brain,
Within Mother, within the blue light; the universe embraces
you in its ordinary arms – as escape's shoreline recedes.

31.3.79 / 29.3.85, Poznań

A Letter of Consolation

Even Magdalena, when we read a letter from you,
binds the words in the dressing of a reply, which we also
                                                    read
to each other. And the South wind accompanies her to the
                                                    North
Of your agony which consumes human thoughts. A reply
                                    dispersing the ashes
Of solitude with the glimmer of a curative smile. Yet it
                                                    cannot
Extinguish the sparks of despair from your eyes. No: nothing
                                                    ever
Begins or ends in time; time does not unravel like a woollen
                                                    thread
In death's labyrinth of sliding walls. He Is the language
In which you learn to breathe the Light that does not flow.
Which Is. And It does not stand still; It breathes you and
                                    me, and Magdalena.
So too your father shines so bright, that there is a black fire
In his eyes. So brush aside time's creeping ivy, tear it away
                                                    from
Death's mirror, and then perhaps you will be swallowed by
                                    the Living Sea.
Perhaps you will even assist us in our despair when – the
                                    Time Comes.

24.2.80 / 11.7.85, Poznań

Tadeusz Żukowski

A Letter to Poets in Flames

They are aflame. True poets burn like human torches.
Those who are still alive and those who aren't. Pits of flame,
Columns of fire: these they are in themselves. Fire, fire,
Fire cleansing deep into the whitest agony: the brain's
self-consuming star. And Death, bearing that star in
its jaws; Death, who impounds the bodies abandoned by
poets

On this shore. Death chants pure fire, whispers intimate
passion

Into lines of poetry, all the while distilling vulgar alcohols
into the kidneys.

Death is as treacherous as bridges, safety lines and the
water's depth

They are torches of loneliness ablaze beneath the surface of
the ice;

Way above them there float the high deserts of the cities
where it rains

From human veins. And no one can help or assist them –
No one. Only the abyss lasts and consumes every step.
Aflame – they depart, only to burn to ashes and leave an
ever deeper Dusk.

18.5.84, Poznań

A Letter Full of the Desire to Move
Mountains

What is this – – a rock expanding up into my mouth , it is –
Not! a mountain rising out from my heart – and it is –
rubble,

Dust – but not a voice!... I do not know how to speak
to You –

Lord, You who are within words, are the Word, beyond it,
Above and through – and it cannot double-cross my thoughts
Or Your Voice – oh, Lord send down the grace of speech
That can hear Your Silence. Wrench from within me
The germ of foolishness, in my lungs burst into flame
With the fire that scorches: turn my throat to ash for the
silence that

Is such a pure, harsh, open crystal of utter sound, that my
mouth's rock

Will burst into blossom and the heart will inhale its burden –
The mountain's core – which like a sheer cliff: is as light as
A star magnified by the seas. In this pool of space cleanse
my countenance. Then

Petrifying for You utterly, I shall leap over the mountains of
– unbelief.

11.11.81 / 27.3.85, Poznań

Katarzyna Boruń

Born in Warsaw in 1956, Boruń did not, despite extraordinary efforts, study at the Academy of Fine Art or the History of Art Department of the University of Warsaw. Instead she attended seminars at the Łódź Film School and in Autumn 1989 was a participant of the International Writing Program of Iowa University. Boruń's debut came with the publication of some poems in *Nowy Wyraz* (New Expression) in 1974. So far she has published the volumes *Wyciszenia* (Quietenings, Warsaw 1977), *Mały happening* (A Minor Happening, Warsaw 1979), *Życie codzienne w Państwie Środka* (Daily Life in the Middle Kingdom, Warsaw 1983), *Muzeum automatów* (A Museum of Automatons, Bydgoszcz 1985), and most recently *Więcej – wiersze o zmroku* (More – Poems at Twilight, Warsaw 1991). Boruń has worked as a messenger, reading room assistant, small ads clerk and eventually became an editor on the monthly *Powściągliwość i Praca* (Temperance and Hard Work).

History

Which one of my friends would still believe in words,
who would nowadays still stitch a demo banner through the
                                                            night,
who would prepare bandages for the struggle by feeble
                                                    candlelight?
and yet I hear that at dusk they practice
recounting their dreams,
in their airtight rooms
humming the ancient songs never taught in schools
whose verses everyone knows
so they do not need to be sung out loud.
Which one of my friends still believe in words;
and yet constantly I see
how by weak light
they breathe into their lungs
the scent of yellowing newspapers
sensing the smell of feathers rustling in the print
and the fluttering of wings against their faces.
Who of my friends still believes in gestures
which have eaten away at their muscles like rust
does into the wood of the cross;
and yet they still sleep vigilantly waiting for reveille
and a half-waking hand searches at their side
for the invisible, well-oiled weapon.
Which one of my friends would still trust the figures
whose names fester on the banners dedicated
to our Fatherland and God.
And yet I see that day by day
they rush faster down these streets as if they were trenches
keeping their heads hunched down into their shoulders
as if dodging the gunfire
murmering the words of a prayer
for their only possible reward – to die in a state of grace.

Katarzyna Boruń

Daily Life in the Middle Kingdom

The Mandarin only responds in monosyllables.
A cat fawns itself onto a twisted tree
(the English disease: splendid isolation).
You who are nailed through your centre of gravity to the
cross

of your Christian mission
you still chase swallows
in the human body's restaurant.
Behind a paper screen
you toss sad mun mushrooms
and bamboo sprouts with your chopsticks.
You make no effort to discern thoughts in the greasy
characters.

The bamboo grows,
and by morning will have torn off our skin,
by noon it will have pierced the heart.
In the evening
in the pale blue opium den,
on small bound feet
a blind female child
mercifully rescued from being drowned
will fawn at your silken slippers.
The Miraculous Mandarin only responds in monosyllables.

'A Sad Song of a Lonely Bedroom'

"Why should I want fire or should I want light?
A purring cat don't take the place of someone asleep
                                    breathing beside,
why should I need a pillow soft under my head
or no traces of loving in my chill big bed".

Sing, now, sing, lady with the long black hair,
the squeaking of your vocal chords cannot fill in the silence
that will fill the space when the drunken rapper
stubs his cigar out on one of the piano's keys.
So sing, now, and let the clarinet's voice
sway in your ears
like a bronze ear-ring
that crumbled to greenish dust deep in the earth long ago
among with the cheap emotions and rhymed lines of the
                                    blues.
So sing out, while someone is still walking over your grave.
The streaks of your hair are as black as the grooves in a
                                    record:
ebony – that sad parody of Africa:
and the black totem that still slumbers within you.
A white critic caresses the legend in his trembling fingers
examines a cheque beneath the light, turns off the
                                    gramophone
and falls asleep alone in the cold bed of an old man.

114

Katarzyna Boruń

Marlowe Private Eye is the Poet of the Night

The gaunt poet carries inside himself a bigger Marlowe.
Just look at that weary cigarette end
stuck to his lips.
Here the poet has
his own minor Sunset Boulevard,
where a cheap soup kitchen, despite the crowds,
has the lonely taste of a Hopper canvass,
where the support services of female intellectuals in
the *boutique*-era
is no less well-meaning than carat-laden millionaires'
wives
and an untried metaphor is no less accurate
than a bullet in the knee.
Phillip M. is only a Private Poet.
The gaunt poet adores Big Marlowe.
Does it matter that the detective doesn't like the poet.
No one likes people hot on the track of the emotions.
Marlowe Poet smiles the tired
scowl of
a ginger cat.

Tosca

You can't really live for art, but you can live well off it.
Formal receptions, celebration performances, charity balls
                              and matinée concerts.
Opera singer is no profession for any decent woman.
In front of orphans I sing as a lovely consumptive,
in front of the chief of police I sing the role of a naive
                                      innocent.
I know that opera singer is not an honest woman's calling,
but then is being a policeman a proper job for a sensitive
                                          lover,
or then is painter the right choice for a true patriot?
But it's always me that has to take centre stage.
I'm the one whose voice gets heard.
I greet every coup d'état with a high C,
and my voice never falters even for my murderous aria.
Scarpia is eating, Mario screams out in pain, and I just keep
                                          singing.

Katarzyna Boruń

The City's Poets Look Down from its Highest Tower

It will be easier for us, it will then be easier
if instead of speaking directly, we pile up the metaphors
and wrap our tongue in poetry's white fleece.
This city that sells itself
for false friendship, for the words
and gestures of tradesmen or pimps
has shut me like a book once more
left read unfinished, has brought me here
to offer me to the river. And then it handed back
again as no one else's to the evil shore.
Look at the townsfolk long since abandoned
to the clutches of its gateways and necropolises.
We do not differ from them at all.
Our home is a dark and narrow trickle of tea spilt
over a tablecloth and a heart
lanced by a Singer sewing machine needle.
Like the newborn
we mill around endlessly
in a monastery cupboard of waifs and strays.

A Domestic Song

You shall have as much happiness
     as the string you can hold in one hand,
you shall have as much warmth
     as there is coal in your cellar
you shall have as much light
     as there are windows in your wall,
you shall have as many enemies
     as you can count.

You shall have the same heart
     with which you were born
you shall have as great a sense of taste
     as there is bitterness in your mouth,
as much freedom
     as there is between one wall and the next,
and only as much hope
     as you can grasp between your fingers.

Your home shall be as high
     as your hand can reach
and your fields as wide
     as the eye can see
and you, woman, shall be your own judge and jury
     your own reward and your own torment.

Maria Korusiewicz

Born in Katowice in 1956, Korusiewicz studied English at the Silesian University, but also graduated from the graphics department of the Teacher Training College in Częstochowa. She mainly works as a graphic artist in book design. Korusiewicz's debut came in 1973 with poems published in the Kraków weekly *Życie Literackie* (Literary Life). Her volume of poetry entitled *Oddział kobiecy nad ranem* (The Women's Ward at Dawn, Katowice 1987) was awarded a prize by the Ministry of Art and Culture. Her most recent volume, *Tajemnica korespondencji* (The Secret of Correspondence, Warsaw) appeared in 1991.

*   *   *

I have this poor sick head again
and behind the pane of glass day stands like a pillar

and I did not pull the curtains, did not close my eyelids
and did not manage to stitch myself tight under the
                                                        bedclothes

I know that I have to sleep have to sleep even when my head
                                                        burns
even when like a slug it slithers up my throat

and when it wants to jump from the top floor
I think suddenly calm down dearest calm down

but once again I have this broken down head
and I have not managed to tie my own hands

and beyond the window like a column like a fork of lightning
like the Empire State Building

like a spear like an archangel like Marylin Monroe
the day stands there

*   *   *

what can a woman be afraid of
who owns the most expensive of shoes

who has considerable achievements behind her
who has no children

who knows how to open a jam jar herself
and to bake a cake

who can walk long distances even after nightfall
who is healthy and can become a cosmonaut

who knows foreign languages
and who knows how to and who can

and who (to be continued . . .) . . .

*   *   *

and so we came to stand at the very edge of the skies and the
                                                        wind
of the blue plains tearing at the wings

of anxiety that had crawled under the blanket and pecked at
                                                        my feet
and now, as an old crow, it squawks buried deep inside

of the bed white with cobwebs
and I lie still inside this wedding bag that is my body

because that must have been a wedding that rape
that sprang from the lair of his mouth like a mouse

gnawing at the eyes at full pelt and now dead and dirty
it lies wound in the sheets after all who's ever seen the skies
                                                        slit open

with a razor blade?

* * *

my face is a mug of black coffee
my face is a hand without fingers
a threatening alarm clock

it does not know how to tick
it does not want to eat
it does not leave the house

I have painted it red and blue
I have dyed its hairs
straightened the teeth

every day a new strip-tease
a grand spectacle
every day it would sing like a primadonna

during the nights it would lick your warm tongue
your warm tongue would dance with it till dawn
at night it grew like a yellow tulip only to

kiss it more and more and more
now it's lying on top of me like a coiled beast
cold and clammy and wet like a jellyfish

now finally you can give it one right between the eyes

*   *   *

I'm thinking of hurting you

that's why I've stopped smoking
that's why I don't look out of the window any more
all that's left is to select the means

I've bought the bath tub
and hung ropes all around the place

I have disinfected my hands
and laid out your Sunday clothes

I have understood the significance of these contractions in
                                    my stomach
and I know why my hair is getting greasy

I have barricaded the doors
and I have loved everything in you
all that is left is to choose

Maria Korusiewicz

The Statue in the Park

hero is pale
a high coarse forehead with a greenish
down of wrinkles a chipped nose
shallow and soft lips, hardly touched by a chisel
a few dried leaves some
grey stone
lying beneath the maple tree's black branches

on the small snow-covered square
the ravens freeze
two broken benches lie at the base of the pedestal
hero's coat hangs wafting in the wind
although snow is falling silently and sensibly
cleanly over the earth

hero is not asleep
does not alter the expression on his face
change his gloves or his horse
the concrete bay horse is always the same one
its knee half-bent
with the hoof chopped off
he points towards the low sky of my block of flats

hero is careful
he does not try to jump aside
he has discreetly lost the legibility of his inscription
he has misplaced the pointing finger of his left hand
he prefers not to remember
the heat of battle the clash of swords

he gives no credence to the fantasies of national poets
or to articles in the daily press or the rather thin
leaflets which they occasionally stick all over his head
he sits straight-backed on history's cutting edge
stubbornly staring at the queue waiting in front of the kiosk
the broken street lighting the cracked paving stones
set against the bruised dark blue sky
the stone body of his dreams is crumbling

Sin's Divine Fruit

Beneath the arches of the severe vaulting
in the pale, unmoving light of the great nave
of the German church
Bernadeta Brolik
fell heavily to her knees
(Behind the bright blue stained glass the snow
lay on the fields
pathways and motorways
all the way to Poland)

The priest raised the chalice and she
(eighty years old and haughty)
in her black boots
her tightly wound bun of thin
grey hair
beats her breasts

for her divorced, off-hand daughters
for her German grandchildren
for the Volksliste she signed furtively
in thirty-nine
in the Silesian town of Patnów
and then
for her contempt and foolish arrogance on the second floor
of the opulent Prussian mansion block where she used to live
and for her terrors

and then additionally for her passions
for ample shiny skirts starched collars
greasy smoked goose breast and half-litre bottles of vodka
bracelets of golden sausages and necklaces
dances lasting till dawn in stifling rooms and lipstick
powders nylon stockings and
that young organist
with the soft white buttocks
who was so expert and later
trembled and perspired in the vestry's shadow

Maria Korusiewicz

Mediaeval siligia
brown streams of festering sin run down
onto a tidy scrubbed tile floor
drip into the confessionals that have been empty for years
stain the woolly permed heads of the old women
from Münchengladbach

The ancient list of slight, venial sins:
the fruit of paradise grown out of the desert's sands
the fruit of the mortifications of Egypt's ancient anchorites
the fruit incomprehensible and irrelevant in the comfortable
ritual of the mass
seeps out into the silence

The gilded angels unfold
their metal arms
the faithful without sound or absolution
swallow the bread and the wine
exchange barely perceptible smiles and careful gestures
in the last but one row of pews Bernadeta Brolik
her hands pressed tight to her breast
with monotonous open eyes
like a weird long-extinct bird
shorn of its wings
kneels
in the silver, inconceivable light
of lamentation

Meditating on the Power of Rome

They caught him out on the white steps of the Senate
the sky was clear and blue alluring
by the trilling of birds and the soft warmth
of the sunlit roofs
Caesar fell
in the midst of raised blades
among swirling cloaks
his balding head slid down
to the stone edges of the inlaid steps

That spring there were two Brutuses
Quite definitely both
were tanned and lean (the murderers of kings
are rarely overweight)
in silver armour
in bleached togas
hips accustomed to a sword hands relaxed
on the handle of a knife
Splendid forty-year olds with the arrogant eyes of the Stoics
(Cicero knew full well with which decorative flowers
Roman nobility likes to decorate itself)
but which one was it
Marcus or Decimus
the taller one or the one in the tunic edged with red
the adjutant or the senator
the victim of Antonius's dexterity or the suicide not far from
                                                    Phillippi
who landed the mortal blow
who won the draw
by some strange quirk of fate

I ask because what would you have been Brutus
without the lips of the victim
without the incriminating credibility lent by his last words
we republicans
have a short memory and we prefer
to adore our emperors

So they went back
to their homes put away their daggers
into their expensive cases let in the dancing girls
and the voluptuous women their bodies brimming with fruit
and valued wines
and then they began to die
like leaves
as the years passed
all slain by the same old enemy

The Junii of the Brutus family
locked
into the same unfinished quotation
all attempts at escape
at regaining their own identities
end in the shameful reversion
to a mock film script
a series of comic strip frames
a scene where they are embraced by a dying elderly man
history's laughter
myth's revenge
– a joke played by the one who got the knife in his back?

Ryszard Grzyb

Born in Sosnowiec in 1956, Grzyb studied from 1976 to 1979 at the State High School of Fine Arts in Wrocław and then from 1979 to 1981 worked in the atelier of the painter Rajmund Ziemski at the Academy of Fine Arts in Warsaw. Founder member of the anarcho-expressionist group of painters and performance artists 'Gruppa' in 1982 under Martial Law, Grzyb also contributed his verse to the group's occasional periodical *Oj, dobrze już* (Alright Then). In addition to 'Gruppa's' collective exhibitions Grzyb has had numerous one-man shows, and so far his poetry has appeared only in *Oj, dobrze już* and in the art catalogue that was a summary of the explosion of the visual arts in the 1980s, *Co słychać?* (What's Going On?, Warsaw 1989)

Rembrandt the Voyeur of Hope
(The Flight into Egypt – a night scene)

Beyond that dark splash stretches a road
longer than Joseph's imagination
only the donkey knows how far
but what of the engraver?

a street lamp supposedly indicates salvation
but how will people without eyes find it?

Mary has the face of a lascivious demon
Joseph the profile of a whipped mongrel
the donkey is depicted most humanly

they will not find the golden horseshoe

van Rijn will die in poverty
he will only curl up his mouth on his final canvas

they still do not know what they are going to face.

1980

Melancholy

Your melancholy is like a hillock
from which you look out over the surrounding areas
and you see insignificant overworked figures
spaced out under the sun's light in a huge expanse
as on a decorative pen and ink drawing
You think that this is China
and you were here once
but it's not really to do with a past dream
there is too much bleached yolk yellow here
and forms highlighted by an exaggerated chimerical line.

1981

The Golden Rain

Will golden rain fall tomorrow which, unseen,
permeates an elephant's eye and a lizard's paw
Can our eyes contain even a shadow of hope
Can we look forward to anything now disaster manoeuvres
                                                              relentless
ahead and behind
while the spirit that crushes what is good remains here inside
                                                                          us
Will golden tears cleanse those who were wronged
Will all things be set right
Will the blessing of asking questions not simply pass us by
so we can die before our time in hopeless struggles
Will it be granted us at least once to love in a way different
                                                              to animals
and believe in our fellow man
Or will we be the children of dusk and chaos inflicting
                                              abundant further wounds
Will we single out in man what is beautiful
or instead list mercilessly what makes him vile
Will we not die slowly day by day of confusion and
                                                              indifference
Are we not becoming the heralds of man's Fall

Ryszard Grzyb

Hell

Not in this world will you wipe the tears from your enemy's
cheek
Not in this world will you lead a blind dog to a good death
Not in this world will a drop of white reach you in the
darkness
Not in this world will joy magnify your heart.

Włodzimierz Pawlak

Born in Korytowo in 1957, Pawlak studied from 1980–85 at the Academy of Fine Arts in Warsaw in the atelier of Rajmund Ziemski. Co-founder with Grzyb of 'Gruppa' under Martial Law, Pawlak also contributed to the group's occasional periodical *Oj, dobrze już* (Alright Then) in the form of intense philosophical essays and poems. In addition to 'Gruppa's' collective exhibitions Pawlak has had numerous one-man shows, and so far his poetry has appeared only in *Oj, dobrze już* and in *Co słychać?*.

To Be Beyond Good and Evil

To want what is now to be always
To be what you are (even if that were just a lonely freedom).
Not to be different to what you are.
Not to want to be *alone*, or with *someone*.
And not to define, and not to judge.

Not to suffer (and so not delight in it).
Not to delight in things (and so not suffer loss).
Not to control everything, or anything.
To know (and not know how you know).
To feel (and not define).
To be (no longer letting fiction create good and evil).

28.12.81

Włodzimierz Pawlak

A Poem With No Title Since a Title Would Get in the Way and Ruin the Whole Thing

This has already happened once. Then there was an
                                        intermission.
Now, once again, we're back to n o t h i n g.

Nothing is not just the hissing of a Beryl 102 TV set after the
                                        national anthem,
it's a separation from myself.
It's the absence of close friends.
It's Kerilov's departure.
It's Hamm and Clov, Pozzo and Lucky, Vladimir and
                                        Estragon,
Nagg and Nell going off, saying it's the end of literature.
("literature saves us by telling lies")
And in any case that's what my unbelief tells me
as does my consciousness,
when I walk down streets and instead of joy or pleasure
I can see this minor apocalypse.
I go back home grasp at words, which until recently
rescued me
and I see that minor apocalypse.
I read them, but books recede
And I am left behind
And as for the uncertainty in the existence of God
my belief in that uncertainty grows day by day.

Well, there's always Robinson Crusoe left
but all islands are full of venom anyway.

So once again there is nothing, the nothing that was here
                                        once before.

7.11.82

139

I Wipe the Red Paint From My Hands

I wipe the red paint from my hands with disgust with
revulsion
then with repulsion I excrete it
I am so profoundly affected by red

I would like to coat everything in white paint
wiping my hands only to frown, submitting to delusions of
eternal artistry

How many more times, to save God, the Spark, the Shaft of
Light,
the Light of the World
Can I keep believing that this is not the way it is at all.

* * *

No one can prevent you asking questions, but who will
                              supply the answers?
The taste of self-denial with the taste of victory (at what
                                            price?).
To eat my fill of potatoes, bread – to take a drink of milk
play with my children,
light up a cigarette, flicking ash over a snow-covered field,
to look for a diamond, there's definitely one among the
                              washed up dishes,
in the dust of the floor that has been swept year in year out,
in the way you come round to accepting the cruelties of the
                                            world
between one piece of chewing gum and the next.
This is where a landscape of thoughts from beyond this
                              world extends out
Between life and death there stretches a land fit
for children, who will do everything in their power to grow
                                            up.
Coming from that place, we now find ourselves here in
                              Frankfurt (at a red traffic light)
with a woman from East Berlin, who cries after drinking a
                              bottle of Champagne costing DM 250.
In front of Warsaw's Palace of Culture and Science
in a Sovtransavto bus filled with itinerant street traders I've
                                            paid a lot less.
How can I explain that the first woman cried twice,
And the second didn't at all?

Day by Day I Get More and More Russian

I soar in the void with long-dead commanders, with literary
figures
I foam at the mouth with froth and sand,
I transgress the borders of the stench of onion, gherkins,
carbide-based home-made vodka
I can see the brilliance of a light bulb
with my head bowed heavy like a goods wagon,
to reveal at every next moment
with a voice just exhumed from the grave
the words that rush to slit my throat
– Lower your head and you will easily forget fields, forests,
dogs.

Zbigniew Machej

Born in 1958 in Cieszyn, Southern Poland where he still lives and works as a secondary school teacher, Machej studied Polish philology at the University of Kraków, making his debut as a poet in 1980 in the sparse pages of the Catholic weekly *Tygodnik Powszechny*. His first volume appeared with the Warsaw publisher Czytelnik (Reader) in 1984, *Smakosze, kochankowie i płatni mordercy* (Gourmets, Lovers and Contract Killers). Then he published two volumes in the *samizdat* press,: *Śpiąca muza* (The Slumbering Muse, Kraków 1988), and *Wiersze dla moich przyjaciół* (Poems for My Friends, Kraków 1988). These were republished in London in 1990 as *Dwa zbiory wierszy* (Two Collections of Verse).

The Song of Him Who Calls in the Wilderness

What can the value be of this exertion
if in my adamant calling to the world –
with the feeble power of lungs and throat,
the futile gymnastics of the tongue,
the trembling of dry lips – I cannot put a stop to
this godless racket, this inhuman
clamouring, squealing and whimpering
and I am merely exacerbating the agony
on my ears, and contributing to the general clamour?

Zbigniew Machej

Welcoming the Queen of Sheba

Can a hand extended in welcome
to touch another hand
not itself express the warm
heart's whole wisdom?
Can wisdom, ideally,
manage without words?
But is that which is dark or
incomprehensible to the senses
that which torments us in or out of our dreams
which gives us no breathing space,
can this be crammed into words?
And what excites true
admiration? An abundance of gold
from Ophir? An array of ivory
brought in from Tarshish
by a fleet of white ships?
What causes you a sharp intake of breath?
Innumerable herds of
oxen, sheep and horses?
Marvellous banquets on the tables?
The aroma of food? The taste of wine?
Floors made of sandalwood
in the tabernacle of the Lord
or in the palace of the king?
Zithers and harps of the musicians,
made of the selfsame wood?
Or rather the touch
of a welcoming hand,
the warm-hearted wisdom
that manages without words?

*   *   *

Let us spare no pains to know the Lord
Before He comes in the brilliance of the dawn,
He it was who hewed us down through His prophets
And in His passionate fire He did drown us,
And with a single word from His lips He slew us
So that our love for Him would not be like unto the clouds
Or like the dew that vanishes anon.

He it was that smote us, laid us down with his rod of iron
Prepared plagues upon our houses
That the light of His Law might shine forth.
He threw us down, and He will raise us up,
Will bind the wounds that He Himself inflicted.
Before He comes in the brilliance of the dawn,
Let us spare no pains to know the Lord.

146

Poems Written into an Album

Think not too much of the past
Let not yourself be confined by yearnings.
Devise new political conspiracies,
initiate a series of erotic intrigues,
do not think back to depleted love affairs.

Acquire new arts and crafts,
gather a portfolio of professional qualifications.
Do a thousand different things,
but at times do nothing at all and just
sit patiently, wait placidly.

Discover this world's foreign parts
but do not count on its benevolence.
Soberly probe its intentions.
Let not your hide be bought
at a price that is excessively cheap.

The world's colours, shapes and tastes
its smells, rhythms and nuances
adopt these with shrewd discrimination.
Occasionally allow these to tempt you
but never ever attempt to usurp them.

Be limitlessly faithful to someone.
Learn the art of dying, of losing everything
and of forgetting about yourself.
Recognize hope in the midst of hopelessness.
Only in this way will you gain everything.

*   *   *

So what remains of that tender love
bled dry by monotony? A bland taste of flowers,
Wilted petals whose haphazard design
embodies that bruised resentment
and ridiculous pathos of marble.
The wrinkles' inept possessiveness
forks out from the corners of
those green, girlish eyes.
That nose, however, stands out as a proud compass,
during the light of day unerringly pointing to
the North Star. Bared in laughter,
put on of course, like putting on airs of pleasure,
those teeth still tempt like snow on the slopes
of mountains in Africa. And that morning glow
on the neck, the outline of shoulders
that defy memorisation, the almond
flavour of those breasts. But more than
anything that profile, the unique source
of inexhaustible joy.
Unfortunately, oh horror, on its far cheek
there are some black scars
overcast further by a tuft of
ginger hair, as twisted and obscure
as a sketch of the cracks
on walls of basalt rock.
Somewhere high above them
the moon also rises
casting a phosphorescent shadow
with its antediluvian
devil's eye.

Zbigniew Machej

*   *   *

The turn of February, March, and the first days of April:
cold ashes, early violets, and lent's forty days.
The rusted-over piping of the taps smells poisonous
and my head erupts with nightly headaches.

Window panes portray the delirious stares of a madman.
Pregnant girls sell vodka in the doorways of tenement flats.
In the churches around the market place mangy gothic
is tortured by the question what have I done to deserve this?

Oh, how horribly spring's early shoots torment us
in this town where cancer's blue tissue spreads.
It induces a yearning to sleep through this time of
                                                    desolation,
since there is no strength for laughter or lamentation.

An Old Prophecy

The time of democracy is upon us, and faith shall prove
to be as transitory as human laws. The expense of renting,
import duties and taxation rates shall be the appropriate
measure
of freedom. Deficits shall dictate new dogmas.
Political vigilance shall deteriorate into unbearable
procedural tedium. Words will nonetheless still
conceal thoughts, and the halo that encircles foolishness

shall never dim. The hands that tore off thorns
shall cleanse themselves before clasping hands that wove
whips. Dignity and desire shall find refuge under the same
roof, and the wolf shall lie down with the black sheep
and the ugly duckling. Dreams of a wholesale business
selling exotic fruits shall eclipse the longing for pure
art. The Messiah of the Lithuanian prophets will find no

refuge, not even in a waxworks museum.
Doubt shall confine the imagination of poets
to the visible, real world. Love,
luckily, will once more dispose
its metres within unpredictable rhythms.
And yet nothingness shall ultimately reveal itself as pure
as the blue sky on a postcard from Rome.

1991

Andrzej Sosnowski

Andrzej Sosnowski was born in Warsaw in 1959. After studying English at the University, he lectured in American literature, and now works in the respected Warsaw publishing house, PIW (Państwowy Instytut Wydawniczy), and contributes to the periodical *Literatura na świecie* (Literature in the World) which translates foreign literutre into Polish. He has published occasional poems in various literary magazines, but his debut came in 1992, when Przedświt Publications published *Życie na Korei* (Life on the Korea Housing Estate, Warsaw). His most recent poems were included in the volume *Dom bez kantów* (The House without Corners, with poems by Kuba Kozioł and Tadeusz Pióro, Moveable Feast Press, Chicago, 1992)

Summer 1987

And so it was that your death took its place in my shadow,
to lean up against me, to breath by means of my thoughts.
I stood up on impulse and searched for the sun at its zenith.
I armed myself to the teeth with humour and vitamins.

I shrugged my shoulders and gave my soul a shake down
I tore off the black bandages, the black halo from my
                                             memory
You gave me my inspiration. I ate fruits by the handful.
All essential minerals held guard over my cells.

I walked dauntless and fast from errand to errand
even jumping into marriage humming epithalamia.
I even began working out: jogging, press ups, sit ups –
but no excess that would favour an early overdose.

But the days went over the top and each ferocious dream
that followed from any aura of visions and shift in thoughts
was like an acute attack on the earth's surface area,
the body pounding to enter its allotted winter plot.

And I was going mad, and lost my loftiness
I lost my pace and mark, and lost my breath –
disastrous poriomania and delirious trips –
not from Bordeaux to Nürtingen, but whatever.

The ground beneath my feet is so soft all around –
I felt my feet sinking into it up to my ankles.
But at night – my bed was like a trap door
and it would soundlessly slide open under my body.

Later there were memory gaps, and gazing through
windows –
there a little girl in the housing block opposite
smiles with a razor blade between her teeth.
I consider the chilling kisses she can give.

Andrzej Sosnowski

A Walk Ahead

Do you deserve the grandiose fiction of this
life without factual details, this overwhelming meaning?
At dusk the megaphones broadcast secrets,
mountainous words over which the sun cannot heave itself
and in this noisy accumulation you listen intently to an
                                                    orchestra
of carnivalesque revelries; jugglers and clowns
make their way down the arteries, bells and cymbals
buzz like a cloud of one day-old mayflies.
And the heart turns about face, and reason dissipates into
nothing as the world goes black before our eyes, and
they weakly vanish, snuggle beneath eyelids, or hide
underneath the eyebrows, for they have had enough,
                                                    really . . .
Assuredly times of happy unknowing are close.
Assuredly you were under some misapprehension if you
                                                    thought
that things revolve around some or other concept of beauty
at its most basic: a cute arse or the political game.
Meaning forces its way through all the doors and windows,
                                                    well,
rather like a stomach pump. Stomach pumps, sewers and
                                                    spittoons,
alliterations, incompetent rhymes, dust and powder
avant tout choses, which always wins out, particularly
when the sun unexpectedly bursts in and makes it all
stand on end like hairs on the skin of objects,
that arietta of nothingness, the auras of things.
So when will I stop falling into those worlds?
It will be when you come down a notch, and spin a finer
                                                    thread,
when peering out of the corner of your eye you double-check
defective landscapes, when you collect scraps of roadside
                                                    jetsam,
then will you locate the point of it all and at that point you
                                                    will
dismiss nature from its post. Then out for a walk

153

with pockets full of cash and perfumed handkerchiefs
just in case. And you enter the evening
as if a soaring avenue, in the darkness the air
thickens with ghosts; their voices palpitate like
the croaking of toads and the lofty hymns of mosquitoes.

Andrzej Sosnowski

Life down on Korea*

Maybe now is the time to resort to happiness,
maybe you won't get pinned to a wall, perhaps
you will not be called to silent account with your lips
clasped tight in embarrassment trying again and again
to explain this anachronism. Only one thought occurs:
your hurried words are a foreboding once more
of baking harvest-times and that ecstacy at dusk
when dancing breaks out, the overwhelming
anticipation of those casual love affairs
that refresh you like a tart apple plucked unintentionally
when walking through an orchard, and biting into it once
you then hurl it far away. And life is surprisingly such an
enjoyable stretching of the self, a protective
yawn at the sun; what, you're here already,
old chap? And you too, my fine feathered friends?
So you are. I suggest a ritual and a prayer
and then start to worry. Let's hope you succeed –
just do not faint on the tracks down which the days
thunder in their shiny sleeping carriages
and the nights stand around in goods trains waiting
for the lights to go green. Reason falls into a light sleep,
the senses having occupied the line and yet again very
beautiful things take my attention: apples, water, milk,
crystal-clear air. Then, once you have taken to heart
that you have certainly not deserved this or any other
quarter

of an hour, you will be able to have a drink or two,
crumple up the world, and, at last,
reflect on it all.

*'Korea' is the local name for a small triangular district in central Warsaw.

Millenium

The millenium is here. Now everywhere and forever
little girls in white and boys in pale blue will process
through the golden towns and smile up at the empty sky.
On the seventh day the rains ceased and queues formed.
The grey clouds fell like musical wallpaper.
Standing right behind you in the downpour of songs,
observing lines of people interwoven with banners and
slogans,
I wonder: are we really standing in line for that ounce of
happiness, for fate cut into thousands of little coloured
cardboard box sized portions, as surely make-believe
as plaques with Allelujah on the sides of housing blocks or
banners
proclaiming the joy and harvest of common sense. And your
response?
"Just like those Indians dozing among the statues
and asleep on the terraces of the overgrown temples,
we discover in the glare of flash-bulbs that history is a variety
show,
the diamond sequins on a celebrity's shoes."
That's as much as she would say. And not a word more,
nothing,
no asking about what to do in these new circumstances,
no demand for an expert opinion. For everyone
expects some obscenity, along the lines of "think
then die", or else the declension the senses down through all
the 'what for' or 'with whom' or 'what?'. So, yes, catch
that first available plane over to Berdyczów or Briliantistan –
we shall surely meet there.

Autumn

They also overstep the measure, mayors and elites,
sending letters full of unrepeatable offers
of life so vertiginous, that the glare on the platforms
plays like a music box and someone guffaws in laughter
when the wind tosses the leaves and reveals the blood
which was hidden by autumnal gold. And so we want to cry
as we suffer sparingly in the midst of innumerable victims.
But someone explains he lives a predatory life
jumping from night into the hurried morning
and someone one evening suppresses a whimper on donning
an ironic smile like a double-breasted three-piece suit.
And only in autumn will you become acquianted with
sleep's ideoplastic, growing on the air's verges:
in girum imus nocte et consumimur igni
(nightly we turn and then are consumed by fire).

What is Poetry?

It is certainly no good as a strategy for survival,
or even a means for living. Your stubbornness is laughable
when you bring to mind the cursed lakes, the deep rustling
forests and deafening caves, in which a voice passes into
                                        echoings
and then certainly rumbles on for aeons. And the Sibylline
caves? Leaves are significant and perhaps so too the rhyme
word – absurd, for every word impress itself upon this world
and absurdity indeed allots each leaf its proper name.
But just attempt to grab hold of one! Just try
to touch the ground and fly further afield
like a smooth pebble skims the water's surface – how often?
Five or twelve? A series of poems and reflections,
a series of leaves, and yet all those pebbles and leaves –
opaque forms – lie one beside the other
in a never-ending tidiness. And then there is the cave
or else the ever-so-small room. What about those wafts of
                                        air!
A draught rushes in as you open the door and the wind
scatters the leaves, and the world stands on its haunches
while words are sent flying like confetti in disarray.
But do not look askance or leave yet
with sullen mouth. Regret no single delay
for perhaps it will sing out itself? Perhaps suddenly
it will describe people and wars, work and travel,
how things stand, how business is doing . . .

And for those who do not know things, images are a
                                        consolation.

Andrzej Sosnowski

An Essay on Clouds [fragment]

Fragments of alien lands and those familiar worlds
in the episodic cloud formations that teach us passivity and
sensitivity to detail: "the smell of elephants after the rains",
the shadows of the clouds and the scent of the light on the
wet grass,
the wise, child-like joy concealed within the emotionality
with which you responded to those beautiful foreign names
Hancock Mountain, Wahiti Rangers – the domains of
revelation?
"We ought to invest our speech with a strange accent –
people are illuminated by what comes from afar".
And when one summer morning you are drinking beer in a
bar
and you are pleased that the mugs are huge, solid jars
that bang down on the tin counter, glistening pipes and
wizards
at pouring glassfuls, and the head you could slice with a
razor blade
or blow up into the air like the head of a dandelion clock –
just think about clouds, raise your sights and look for a good
long while at those cumuli, until the world below begins to
sway.
"So what will this utterly new world taste like?"
that thought goes straight to the head like beer on a
sweltering day.
Bitter, sweet, then bitter again and the relief of pleasure
as if you'd swallowed the sun like an aspirin and soothed
your throat swollen from an excess of obvious problems –
out of reach of all suns, the clouds remain up there,
ribbons, wreaths of steam and configurations of air
with their superficial movements that are only soundless,
initially light and wind, then necessarily the clouds
themselves,
not as decoration but as a unique exploration.
A single cloud came to mind and eclipsed my sins.
The naked eye needs to discard the sharp contours of things
and relax in that expansive knowledge, the breath of clouds.

"For three days we waded through the dense vapours,
the frost glued our eyelids together and froze our breath
though the sun hung just beyond the wall of whiteness.
We walked along the knife-edged ridge, and then down the
                                                    rainbow
as if on skis parting the air with forehead and neck
we travelled swiftly down through the iridescent sheets,
through the panes of air, only to fall after a moment
into the snow's hard quilts that injure the hands.
"Discover the physics of the wind's mineshafts,"
said the Master, crawling out from under the powder snow
"so each and every thing has its own quantity, scale and
                                                    weight."
Drops of water and ice's microscopic crystals,
the freezing of steam and water's condensation –
the sweeping of mist up to heavens, such is the mystery
of the extensive landscapes of the troposphere's orchard.
Stratus, Cirrus, Nimbus are much like its fruits
as are corpulent Cumulus and its subcategories,
Cumulonimbus or Cirrostratus.
In other words: swirling swishes feather-lined,
laden with rain or arranged in layers
above and below the airline like icebergs,
wedding dresses or huge shoals of fish.
But beware their playful forms and deceptive colours
lest the mind melts into pure cloud
or stardust from the trenches of the stratosphere –
a radiant or even iridescent cloud.
Remember Hamlet: more than one storm-cloud
has led dreamers astray from their chosen path."

Death of a Formless Person

That means yours: so just smile at its stipulation
to keep things simple, hold the body still
and set the soul in motion, because the head's giddiness
is unlike former ones: not the deep sleep in winter
like ski jumping on mammoth take-off
or spring's own momentum: a flare, a dancer's veil
shooting into the darkness, after which you slid down
the chute that apparently ends up in summer's swimming
                                                    pools.
How long can you drift along the lines?
You box with shadows and after a direct punch lands
you fly off somersaulting into the expanse between the
                                                    stars –
the world whispering at your back like an avalanche out of
                                                    breath.

And renouncing all things can you cope with nothing to do
stranded as a lonely tourist on a cloud? We made "yes, yes"
                                                    noises
during the good times, and as things got worse it changed to
"any time, any place". And it does get worse:
you sit down in the dust next to a suburban wall
throwing stones like a redundant suitor
you stare at the clear sky recalling the clouds and
the storms of long-past situations and tempestuous
                                                    meanings.
And at night your light attracts the world and nothing else –
only moths knocking against the window pane and a cricket
as if someone were stomping around in buckled shoes
I should so like to be the victim of a unneccessary intrigue.

Marcin
Świetlicki

Marcin Świetlicki was born on Christmas Eve 1961. Associated
with the 'new wave' of 'Barbarian' poets who publish in the
Kraków-based quarterly *brulion*, and some of these poems also
appeared in the 'Barbarians' group anthology *Przyszli barbar-
zyńcy* (The Barbarians Have Arrived!, Kraków 1991). His volume
Zimne kraje (Cold Countries) was published by *brulion* in 1992.
He works on the editorial board of *Tygodnik Powszechny* (The
Catholic Universal Weekly).

* * *

Why is it your anxiety revolves so around
words like: prisons, uprisings,
west, east, freedom, food,
access to this or that,
political
prisoners?
These are small words, these are the smallest of words,
why is it that your tongue has got caught in them?
Don't you know that all of this is
under the control of a rather slinky tart
the one you love, or rather fancy –
who actually chooses the person detested
by you, the one who mistreats her and hammers the nails

into her

because of her you are in this prison,
because of her you are hungry.

The Town of Słupsk, 1984

October's sharp air
would taste better in a different town to this.
Just to get onto an empty night tram
doze next to your own dozing coloured reflection
in the misted-up window – to travel, to doze.
Instead I sleep in an eight-bedded dorm
and carry out the orders of these brutes.
Here, in this vile place, it is easier to see twilight,
blades of grass, rainbows. With utter awe, volcanoes astound
those touched by their lava fingers.

Battlefield

She's lying here next to me. She's pretending to sleep.
Will anything beautiful be left after all this carnage?
We've already killed off everything. Bright moths
touch against the window panes from both sides. Peace.
For the moment it's all quiet.

She's repeated a hundred times or more she doesn't want
                                                    me.
So I've tried every human ploy. And she's still here. Here
beside me on a put-you-up bed at a friend's.
She has lost. She has her victory. So have I. But I've lost
                                                    too.

She's lying there. I'm dressed now – sitting out of
the way. I watch her and smoke. And stare.
Two glasses of tea, overturned, cracked.
One ashtray, and in it two cigarette ends.
When she opens her eyes I'll open fire again.

Marcin Świetlicki

The Truth About Trees

trees do not have their own holy book
trees have more than enough light air and rain
thin branches stretching up to heaven

the heaven of trees is green powerful fragrant
the creator of trees is as green and powerful as them
their creator has not devised a hell for trees

there is no sin there is no obligation
it's enough to exist rustle stretch
it's enough to grow aspire branch out

the creator of trees did not invent a hell for them
particularly fascinating is the trees' tender indifference
with which they accept humans hung from their lower
                                                    branches

¿Le gusta este jardin?

When I take off my dark glasses
The world I'm in is even more terrifying.
But it's real. The true colours
are creeping into their proper places.
A snake slithers over everything that it encounters. It
has touched us as well.

Snow falls and covers everything.
The city is as yet still visible – a black
skeleton illuminated here and there by the headlights
of small cars, I have sat down at a good vantage point
and I watch. It's evening. All the fun fairs
are closed down now.

Evening. Men return with their spoils.
Zealous priests only capable of saving
themselves. A dog walked next to us for a while
and stank. My personal documents
have disintegrated. Everything I loved
has disintegrated. But I'm still in one piece.

There's nothing about me in the Constitution.

1986

The Work Ethic (24 March 1988)

I am sweeping the stairs leading up to the
Palace of Arts. This is no metaphor:
it's the real thing. Extra cash.
Poetry needs to make its living somehow. Poetry
has to eat.
It's spring. The winter has left behind its dirt –
this white stuff so easily transubstantiated into wet,
dark and sticky ooze. A mass
of cigarette ends, papers, bird droppings, dog turds and that
one is probably excrementally human.
That is no metaphor either: it's the real thing.
My use of words has brought me
to this place. It's clouding over.
Rain won't wash off everything.

An Apocryphal Tale

The Little Boy Jesus was an unbearable child.
It was immediately obvious that he wasn't all there.
A flock of old biddies earnestly debated his nature
making the sort of superstitious gestures then in fashion.

The child possessed an extraordinary memory
remembering exactly the entire order of the galaxy
and he applied it in his very own
long-suffering and incomprehensible way.

He ran with a stick in his hand among his fellow children
and began to organise revolution
or transformed the malicious old biddies
into birds and mosses.

His parents often took him to one side
and looked at him with great distress
then he raised his finger in warning
and sheepishly they returned to their own business.

Now he hangs on walls between the flowers
and over the beds of school-going girls
he has been confiscated by those same biddies
and he is abused by men in black dresses.

But all this, so it seems, doesn't worry him much.
He sits on the edge hitting one stick against another.
One star falls then another
rises.

1988

Opposites

This is how
I imagined hell: beyond its small doors of a fire
there are glowing figures, no longer recognizable,
different hues of burning flame, in front of that fire I could
hold out longer than I managed in front of a TV screen.
I felt I was the grand proprietor of everything
shovelling coal in the shape of the earth's globe through the
open doors,
watching it burn, getting into a fever because
of it.

In my feverish state I walked through my room, passionately
opening one drawer, then more than one at a time
dipping my hands in bravely – brave
because in any one of the drawers I might find
the shards of a mirror – or some old
razor blade of my father. The drawers in that house
were exceptionally dangerous, everything
could reveal a terrible secret: for example
that my parents had kidnapped me from the Gypsies.

I could not fit my mirror-image to
anything or anybody. I assumed that
I had been despatched on some as yet
undisclosed mission which would only
be made known to me once I was
grown up. The hellish fever
gave way to a more run-of-the mill type
so I went back to bed. Along the walls there moved
slow and disturbing disembodied shadows
with huge eyeballs.
Now that I live inside the fire's doors
– in the cold and darkness, now that I am finally
adult, and the true proprietor of everything
– I peer back through the half-open doors at the room to see
how it is slowly turning a fiery red, how glowing coals
cover the charred remains of table, chairs and bed.

For Jan Polkowski

It's time to slam those thin cardboard doors and open up the
windows

to open the windows and air the room.
We've always been lucky, but now luck has
run out. Except in such cases
where poems leave
a stench behind them.

The poetry of internment lives on because of an ideal,
but ideals are the watery substitute for blood.
Heroes were in prisons
and workers are ugly but emotionally
convenient – to internment's poetry.

In internment's poetry trees have crosses
inside them – beneath the bark – made of barbed wire.
How easily the prisoner completes the hellishly
long and virtually impossible journey from writing
to God, it lasts a moment,
like spitting – in the poetry of internment.

Instead of saying: my tooth hurts, I'm
hungry, you and me, the four of us,
our street they say quietly: Wanda
Wasilewska, Cyprian Kamil Norwid,
Jósef Piłsudski, the Ukraine, Luthuania,
Thomas Mann, the Bible and *de rigueur*
something in Yiddish.
If here in Kraków there was still a dragon
they'd congratulate the dragon for being there – and then
scurrying away

into their tiny clandestine cells they'd write some poetry
– raising their fists to threaten the creature's very existence
(even love poetry would be set
in dragon type . . .)
> Well, I look hard into the dragon's eyes
and I shrug my shoulders. It's June. That's obvious.

Just after twelve there was a storm. Dusk will first fall
on these ideally rectangular city squares.

1988

Rags

The boys founded a new town.
One hundred worked on its construction, one looked on.
Then he chose its coat of arms and flag,
codified the regulations
– and at that point we stopped belonging
to the same generation.

*

Click. Click.
Haircutting.
A theatrical slaughter.
And mummum the clothes shout
sent off in paper bags.
And mummum the herd calls out.

*

I'm walking alone (covered) in a white sheet
across the marching square.
Sometimes we are the wind.
Sometimes we are a bird,
a sailing ship and a kite.
We flutter a lot.

*

Knock. Knock.
A wooden dais
standing on the asphalt.
And we're in fours.
The back rows are fainting.
Wave
after wave.

*

But the colonel was never a private,
and even if he was – that's just mythology.
When someone asks the question Who didn't volunteer?
– it's not a forest of hands raised, only mine

goes up – and silence – and through the window
(i can) see the colonel standing alone on the dais
he has the same eyes as the eagle hanging behind him.

*

I am the soldier of Another Army
I feed on a different bread.
My head moves my lips
on a group photograph.

*

Intimate smaller worlds.
An ant escapes under a leaf.
The incomparable orderliness of the grass.

*

Tearing out the weeds along a trench
I find the fields of a butterfly:
it hasn't yet lost its colouring.
It only lasts for a moment.
Now
the wind.
I could have made someone pregnant in the same space of
time.

The seconds would be
shorter,
hot
and more lively.

*

Birds are the servicers of our machine guns.
Yellow shimmerings among the trees.
On the exercise yard I have a ring of grass and I crawl.

*

We're warm here
under these grey blankets.
At this moment some of us
are being betrayed
by girlfriends, others though
will be betrayed later on.

*

This is as much as I see when I shut my eyes:
a green square – a cemetery, above it a flock of seagulls:
grey, irregular, ruffled feathers. Now
lifting off, and now landing.
One of the last civilian views
from a train window. This joyous chaos.
I am pleased
when I shut my eyes.

*

In my dreams there are still continuously civilian images:
That civilian air and civilian dirt
under my fingernails – and civilian too
is that not shaving in my dreams, and civilian problems.
In my dreams there remains still
that most clear of clarities.
Outside however, the bells are already ringing. Reveille?
Outside the greenery is bleeding, the rocks are rolling,
one hundred voices in me, over me, in front of me.
The slow hostile sun.

*

The old man likes to warm himself next to the cat.
The old man sometimes hits the cat in the face.
The old man gets emotional in the evenings
when he reads the letters from his cat's fiancées.

*

This must be the most beautiful sentence:
Colonel,Sir,
First Cannoneer So And So
Requests Absence
Requests Absence.

*

Swearing the oath of allegiance.
Everyone's turned up –
parents, sisters, girlfriend. Jack

and Rick. It's like at a funeral.
I was standing in line, but I didn't
even move my lips.
Just a pity, really, that no one
spotted my crime.

*

A butterfly has landed
on my rifle's barrel.
It's all true.

*

You enter the gym
as if it was a church hall.
I take off my beret with its eagle
and sweep, and sweep
under the altar
– an enormous sign with the results of a match:
HOME: GUESTS
Outside the window is the night-time green, it's still there
my eyes wander off.

*

There is no right or left.
My mind streams down the middle.
My wrong right.
My mind streams down the middle.
And you can hear the quiet splashes
and the silent knocking.
I'm a single leg on a centipede.
I'm a single leg on a centipede.

*

This is the only peaceful spot.
STAR WARS. – The heading in a newspaper.
The Japanese with brass kettles on their heads.
A New Zealand surprise raid hangs hidden.
But I am quietly occupying this cubicle, one per one
hundred men. The one and only. Having hung my belt

177

over the door to show it's taken, I am occupying
this space. I don't even pull my trousers down.
I sit, shut my eyes. I don't think of anything,
of anyone. I occupy this
area, when right now
the whole platoon wants to take a shit.

*

The only thing that's happening here now
– is the darkness. JW 2459, Morag. Night.
I woke up screaming. Like, I'd dreamt
that I was locked inside a cross. Inside a cross. Yes.

*

Rags. My God, rags. Strips of pyjamas, strips of cloth
– and the ones that the colour has gone from –
damp and feminine.
I'd like to die – and I don't, don't want to die at all. Kneeling
I rattle off a prayer, screw widows down in my
love poems and I imagine to myself
bits of conversations, I tell myself the plots of books and
films
I hum STRAWBERRY FIELDS FOREVER – and
I admit, while all ancient crimes
are as far off as the signals from beneath the earth's surface,
I don't dare raise my eyes, to look at the corridor
from a mouse's perspective . . .
Rags. Getting out to smoke a cigarette at night
senselessly I bend down
as if I were gathering strawberries.

1984

Jakub Ekier

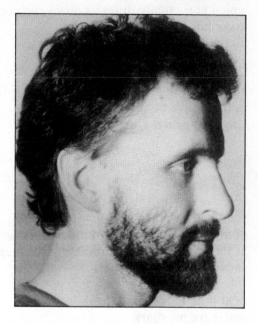

Jakub Ekier was born in Warsaw in 1961, and studied German and Polish at the University of Warsaw. Between 1987 and 1991 he worked as a sub-editor for the Czytelnik publishing house in Warsaw, was a member of the editorial board of Tygodnik Literacki for a short period; now he works free-lance. Ekier made his debut in *brulion* in 1990, and his first volume appeared in their 'library', entitled *cały czas* (the whole time) in 1992. He is a translator of German poetry: a volume of the poems of Rainer Kunze appeared in 1992.

Preface

meadows sloping down under the sky
indefatigable cities infallible tracks that
which perpetually drags us down and someone patient
as air has guided me
all the way here

*   *   *

in the simple incurably broken
language which

is

*   *   *

yet again I walked
in my sleep up to my own mountain pass
at the rocky needle I turned into the eternal
snow

next time I
will leave my mark

*   *   *

he who is unforeseen again initiates
himself and us

*   *   *

inlaid with silence
grey-haired
day

whatever you see
excites your
tranquility

*   *   *

the end of the line
is still far off
in a dark compartment
its head resting
on my shoulder
the world has fallen asleep

*   *   *

yes
now
when the world is standing still
at its full when things are only
themselves when I touch
everything
and it touches me

*   *   *

I enter I leave
while he
with his face turned down to the ground
permanently over me

works

*   *   *

       to Maciej

it will all be sorted out
into a clear-cut pattern

all you need
is to withdraw a little

*   *   *

don't be afraid
look! someone has again overturned
the snowy hourglass so there isn't
any more again

*   *   *

on
you will go without a word
without this poem without yourself

*   *   *

ever more silently
to the frontier of
speechlessness
then along its border
for the whole time

Krzysztof Koehler

Krzysztof Koehler was born in 1963. He is associated with the 'new wave' of 'Barbarian' poets who publish in the Kraków-based quarterly *brulion,* Koehler published *Wiersze* (Poems) in Kraków in 1990. Some of these poems also appeared in *przyszli barbarzyńcy*, and in the Kraków quarterly *Na Glos*.

Ovid. The Last Years.

Black waves smash against the high shore,
Ever more clouds hang high over Tomi,
Soon a storm will descend from the bruised, blue mountains
And forms will dissolve into the night gloom.

Yet thoughts still play with the ripples of words
And fingers quickly drum out a rhythmic phrase.
Don't insult the ears of the gods or Augustus with
too insistent pleas. Take care since a No

Might condemn one here forever. To the edge
Of the world. The sea takes on the grim expression of
                                                        despair.
The coarse grunts of barbarian speech.
Hopelessly empty days and nights of exile.

The elegant arrangement collapses into a whine.
It is more and more difficult to care about appearance.
Filth and feeling forgotten sculpt this alien landscapes
A chasm of disgust deprived of sunshine's sense of scale.

An August Pastoral

Early Autumn. The poplars shed their
leaves and the afternoon sky
pales like a condemned man standing
in front of a firing squad.

The forest brushes
delicately against the horizon,
the air stands still like a stammerer
confronted by a consonant.

Summer is burning itself out
suicidally. The grasses have yellowed.
From now on time bestows
a merciless ripening

on endurance as apples
redden, fate takes satisfaction
in the rustling of the leaves, and the
blowing of the wind,

the dry touch of thoughts
and even rounded, fragrant
sentences. One after the other
like water drops or the ticking

of a clock, a pear tree drops its load.
The plum-tree exudes its juices.
Bees buzz and swarms of
flies drive away approaching voices.

Lines of verse evaporate. The glow
penetrates them, sweat glues eyelids together, and
like Castor and Pollux, shirts are fused
against the body, as if someone

were wounded in the chest, like
a consumptive or a confessor.

There were to have been flocks of sheep,
shadows and fires on the hilltops:

nature *à la fin de siècle*,
but here –
waves break against the shoreline,
a ship shudders,

a dog moans, and very occasionally
the sound of a word draws out
its own shadow – silence again, so
voices subside ever more richly

into whispers. Senility is forever
sending young regiments into battle
as the fullness overflows.

One snake silently slithers past
and arches its Roman nose
that is Augustus's month.

Crucifixion

It was somewhat half-heartedly that the soldier
used his lance to support rather than pierce that man's side
"A static scene. Any mother's heart will comprehend
in an instant that gesture of Mary's hand."

He said. But I was watching John:
off to one side, he outclassed the soldier
with the tone in his eyes, with the gesture of his hand:
"Let there be peace. He has given up his soul

To God." Is this perhaps the source of the Gnostics,
that is, if any one of them ever spent any time in Biecz.
The body does not suffer. The spirit is a separate state.

And Mary Magdalen was also there.
He had nothing to say about her. She was like the earth.
Christ was like time.

Dante and the Poets

They were five, and the wanderer made six.
What they spoke of, he would not deign to say
As they faced the road, which placed in their mouths
The seals of an unfathomable, yet fearful future.

With a sense of foreboding about things for which the time
will come for poetry to speak out, things mean so little that
they can simply be thrown to the mercy of their times.

What is left unsaid today will explode in a scream
And the hungry eye of things swarms over what comes
Next, as that book fell to the ground
When fate carved out a seal from the words of a romance.

Ulysses and Penelope

For K.

Speak softly. It is June, here are the hills.
The year exaggerates the shadows of our
Bodies. Hands. Lips. A white forehead.
A light breeze then, and the smell of fields.
Ridges accumulate step by step.

The cities have been destroyed. Weeds
Have overgrown the streets.
The greying art of navigation still miscalculates.
Joy and fear, like an inheritance, are here with us.

One wave bursts after the last one.
Say this: Let dusk fall and
Seagulls screech. For what has been,
what awaits us, what is here now let
kisses stream on murmuring quietly.

Kraków

I lifted my eyes and slowly into the space
of my room cluttered with things there entered
a silent, majestic tune from the church tower
as crystal clear as a mountain stream.

Before I could cover my eyes there followed
The accompaniment of loudly clanging bells
And the towers of all the churches hereabouts
Chattered away at that hour of dusk

Until the sounds died out. So only the echo carried
Like the noise of battle brought in from far away, when
The wind blows over to an army waiting to face its fate,
Its high spirits and deepest fears, its anger, and its hope . . .

Wilanów

to Barbara Toruńczyk

One bird's exotic cry. The splashing of ducks.
Agitated by some unexpected steps.
An expanse of sadness. Greying rows of willow trees.

A palace looms up through a rainbow. The fountains were
                                                    silent.
Intentions were left unsatisfied.
The wave delicately slid into the shore.

The clamour of the city. Malevolent chimney stacks.
Magically contorted bodies of fauns
And nymphs are overgrown with mosses.

Indulgent forms of trees and bushes.
Beyond the water a forest dallied defiantly in the distance.

All that remained was to look courageously out towards
The other side and tap the dry rhythm out in silence
With one's shoe. The first blossoms

Were bursting out on the trees. A wind was blowing
And leaves rustled – leaves? – the shadows of leaves,
On our way. I also had to follow in their footsteps.

2.

Where ever the poet entered at a slow pace,
The gardener was computing the distances between trees
On his fingers, fountains overflowed with octaves of droplets.
And when it rained then a downpour added to the rainbow.

Where have the Chinese temples and pagodas gone,
And the allegories of the four seasons on the walls
And the ceilings decorated with the outlines of mountains
And plump female bodies. Fanfares.

191

The dull scent of wax and the wizened stream of sunshine
Through the viewfinders provided by door-frames
And hurtling pirouettes performed by the cupids.
Tulczyn, Niemirów or Versailles – interrupted dreams.

This is now another season. Laughter is dozing here.
Pearly chimes of the clavichord, wigs, beauty spots,
The mad chases down tree-lined avenues
And the reverberation of Mozartian tunes.

It is essentially a question of numerals, of addition.
The power of arithmetic and disintegration.
With his fingers the poet taps out syllables in time,
Then praises its passing and drinks more wine.

3.

I wandered around the park. I touched statues.
I investigated the taste of the fountains' water.
I have lost the measure of things. The bells' sounds
Have changed into song. I listened to the bells.

I have lost the measure of things. Its rhythm is too
disconnected.
Dust and rubble poured through my fingers,
And I saw around me rubble and dust, and death,
The unceasing running of water.

A sound too soft. The heart's speech too
Lightweight. Rhythm has sunk beneath the waters.
Fallow springtime has scattered
A fiery rainfall of flowers.

Jacek Podsiadło

Jacek Podsiadło was born in 1964 in Szewna in the Kielce region of Poland. In the mid eighties he worked as a steeplejack for a steelworks in Ostrowiec Świętokrzyski, but between 1989 and 1993 was 'without permanent abode or employment'. His debut as a writer came in 1984, publishing in such magazines as the underground *Wolność i Pokój,* which was set up by peace and anti-militarist activists under Martial Law, but also in other publications like the quarterly *brulion.* Podsiadło's first poetic work was called *hej!,* published in Katowice in 1987, followed by *kompot z orangutana* (Orang-Utang Compote, Elbląg 1989), and culminating in the volume *Wiersz wybrane 1985-1990* (Selected Poems, published in the *bibLioteka brulion,* 1992). Though mainly working as an occasional labourer, recently Podsiadło has started a regular spot on local radio in the Opole region, dealing with the origins of folk and country music. He is not connected with any groups at all.

Song of Our Lady of the Water Closet

I'm so happy
I'm eighty years old
God has forgotten about me
I just have to make sure there's toilet paper there
in its right and proper place

I'm so happy
I'm eighty years old
God has forgotten about me
I just have to make sure there's toilet paper there
in its right and proper place

7.8.86

Two Casual Labourers, Having Put Down their Forks, Stretch Out on the Hay, Turn their Unshaven Faces to the Sun, and are Talking Away Lazily

"During summer time I made myself
like, a geezerber, y'know, taking black plastic bags
then sorta four tyres at the corners, so I never got rained on.
It was cosy, specially when I brought in some hay an' I'd lie
there for days on end. They gave me social security, so I
could live on it.
So can't you get yourself security or somethin', if you've got,
like,
kidsofreania?"

"They can go an' screw
their bloody social security. Like right now
I'm standing on me own two feet. An' when I can't work any
more,
I'll just walk into the middle of some field, find a deep pit an'
just die, right."

"Look mate, this is your Western world, this is,
they're not gonna let you die here. They'll pull you outa the
hole
an' put yer into some home for gerryatrix."

"But I'm only twenty-four."

"You'll be'round a while yet. Like, if you've got
kidsofreania,
an' you ain't got no place, they'll get yer one or another."
"I'm gonna build me one a' them *geezerbers* too.
Used to hang round the railway station, but the fuzz don't
half
bugger things up. With no place to go, well shit, that's no
fuckin' life."

13.4.88

195

*   *   *

To see a teacher
in each one of these three candles
in the toy pistol lying beside me
in these 'Yugo' cigarettes, in a cup of coffee, in Mukunda's
                                        checkered blanket,
in the lunatic teachers of childhood.
To write a poem. To keep watch.
To be next to you with the presence that does not recognise
                                        miles.
To remember the wise teachers too. To be shocked
that wars are still going on, that it's Heidegger who exists
                                        and not nothing,
that Truth plays hide and seek with poetry.
To be the master of surprise. To attribute every belief you
                                        have
to exhaustion.
To travel in time with that small space,
to rock on top of the camel that is your biro.
To love you with words.
That is all that I can manage tonight.
And to blow out those three candles, one by one,
and then, myself, the fourth.

9.1.87

Instead of Complaining, Here's a Better Offer No Cowboy's Girl Can Refuse

Just remember you've got to have a sideboard. Your world
                                   may just fall apart
but there'll still be the sideboard. 'All you need is' a
                                   sideboard
& lots & lots of pots & pans, which are easier to fill up than
a vacuum is. Don't you worry now, we've put Jesus, Gandhi,
                                   King, Lennon out
of their misery, like all the other trash, so our towns are
                                   cleaned up now,
the flower children have wilted, the diamonds belonging to
                                   Lucy as she ran across the sky
have turned out to be junk, & Greenwich Village is squarer
                                   than the Tretiakov Gallery
& no more smelly hippies eager to pick up hitchhikers in the
                                   spirit of apathetic Love.
Throw their filthy books out onto our elegant skip
Ken Kesey the lunatic, Tim Leary the drug addict &
                                   Kerouac the thief,
guys like that are only still fashionable in Eastern Europe &
                                   the Philippines.
Yeah, just buy yourself a sideboard & lots of crockery, a
                                   silver service & video cutlery,
all kinds of drinks, four limousines,
seven hundred pairs of underwear & a bobsleigh track
you've got to achieve something in life.
Make money, not love.
Your cowboy drives a Toyota, he's really cool, trust him,
he'll drive you through life so carefully,
 that you can avoid opening your eyes at all.
All you need is a sideboard.
Don't open your eyes, at any moment something could fall
                                   apart,
better not to look. It'd be easy to lose faith
in the meaning of life, & life has to have meaning:
for example looking after a sideboard.

Be on your guard, some Czech or Hungarian writing poems
for you

is already attempting to carve his heart filled with crap into
the polished veneer.

17.5.88

Don't Leave Me

Don't stop loving me. Not even for a second. Think of me
morning & evening, & when praying. Even at the cost of
                                            missing a meal
even if it means you lose more weight. Feel free, watch
'Dempsey & Makepeace', look at the displays of dresses in
                                            the shop windows,
the symptoms of any disease
on your body – but just hold me in front of your eyes.

Shifting fifty kilo bags of cement I carry you in my arms.
Skipping to a reggae tune I jump after you into the fire.
Biting my nails I bite them out of longing for you.
Listening to the weather forecast I strain to hear your voice.
Sometimes I'm gasping for air
& then I know you've forgotten about me for a moment.

2.2.89

For a Woman Painter

Night has softened & the landscape twitters wildly via the
                                        dark birdlife,
I'm writing this poem for you on an empty stomach, the
                                        unneccessary sun has risen

& above the line of the horizon it has placed its 'pinxit'
                                        crookedly.
The stub of your body at dawn makes its mark in italics

I still have the taste of make-up in my mouth, my obsessive
                                        brain is going to some effort
to work out how to connect the end of the world with the
                                        end of this poem, since
everywhere there's laughter.

But we'll survive this day too, perhaps one day we'll even
                                        have a good
time on this world, which is expiring beneath our feet.

14–15 May 1989

Jacek Podsiadło

Even the Mirrors Will Be On Our Side

we've got to get out of here it's no fun here any more we've
                                                        got to
break the ring of encirclement & take the world
by surprise from behind like a woman we've got to
take it alive with its plants & birds
with its Wimbledon lawn courts mown to medium height
with its lakes scattered around the Mazurian
countryside like silver ducats with its wild Siberian landscape
& the beaches of Port of Spain filled with the queues of
calypso dancers we've got to spend lots of time in the sun
on Jupiter's moon & then on Mars to land on the earth
with a radical sect of Venusian sluts to shout Free
Nelson Mandela & pour a soupçon of johimbina powder
                                                    into the
priests' communion wine – which would make a horse stand
on its hind legs – & then plunder the churches in the name of
                                                    the Holy
Requisition & then burn marihuana mixed with washing
                                                    powder
on piles of banknotes it's got to be a laugh, such a laugh
that Boris Vian turns in his grave onto his left side
& begins to write about us in that uncomfortable
position much as the lives of the saints or some or other daft
                                            stories dreamt up
at his decomposing fingertips how we clambered onto the
                                        colossi on their clay legs
& set off at camel's trot from La Mancha to fight helicopters
how we sailed across the hills from Pachitea in Ucayala
how they wanted to arrest us near Stalingrad because of our
                                                    dress sense
& for tradition's sake & how led by Hašek we escaped
so splendidly, as splendidly as you can only escape from a
                                                    battlefield
& just like Patten got some unchewable gum just as a
                                                    warm-up
because as usual he was trailing at the end playing the
                                                    underdog

201

& how in front of the conscription panel it turned out that
                                        everyone
of us had lacquered toenails & like at the barber's
the mirrors were on our side when they wanted to
deprive us of our long hair & how the Statue of Liberty
                            moaned with delight
when gang-banged by us one after the other & then at
                                        random
all this goes on this is the life we were created to live
only we have to get out of here I can already hear the
                            paranoid voice of
the paragod paraphrasing our poems throw away the pens
                        hands on your head & out

6.6.89

Jacek Podsiadło

Song of My Own Warsaw

Night lays a black plaster on the city's open wound,
the lilac & jasmine in the parks is as fragrant as if a perfume
                                        bottle got knocked over,
a student glues & then rolls out the silent frozen
pastry features of some scapegoat stuck in the poster
of some new political line, a senatorial candidate
being praised for his soft-heartedness & impulsiveness.
Rain thoughtlessly washes the faces of other candidates off
                                        the fence,
though tearing them down before the campaign has ended is
                                        a fineable offence.
The tram is heading back to the depot for the night, its
                                        driver swearing at me
because deep in thought until the last moment
I'd been standing on the edge of the pavement. I just stuck
                                        up my arm at the elbow
though on evenings like this it's pretty easy to get things
                                        wrong:
a step in the wrong direction, the tram's warning bell rings,
                        some pedestrian screams, & it's all over.
All there would be left afterwards is the sense of loss. The
                        person & the suit will be sorely missed.
I quickly bend down to pick up my own shadow lying on the
                                        pavement,
tie it to my ankles, & run diagonally across the roundabout,
repeating an address to myself: Nurska Street Seven Seven.
No thoughts squeeze through the tight gaps between those
                                        four words.
I've got to restrain the instinctive reflex, as my mind wraps
                                        my heart in a heavy rug
& sends it to sleep like a baby, just when it wants to go
                                        crazy.
Some exhibitionist in a shadowy doorway boasting a shiny
                                        pale face
waves something impressive at me while as a policeman
                                        steals an illegal
snooze in the guard's box positioned in front of the Afghan
                                        embassy –

if the queer only knew, he could have penetrated an
                            unguarded building.
I run skipping through the puddles. I jump from one
                            extreme to another.
First it's the metaphysics of excess, & then I've got a deficit
                            in the body stakes.
I know that she'll treat me with her measured tenderness.
She's not even that concerned about the time I get there.
                            She's been ironing.
Blouses, panties, trousers & dresses are piled high on a
                            chair.
There's a new picture decorating the wall, a magic ring with
                            an eye
coloured peach blossom. On a light blue background. Kind
                            of beautiful
but you can tell it's concealing something from the human
                            eye.
When you can see things as if in the palm of your hand,
                            that's when
a new, higher mystery is created. One that's half-joyous,
                            half-vicious.
When my girl scratches me lightly behind the ear & repeats
that it's time to forget about that other world, I feel down
& miss something, though I'm supposed to feel free now
& involved in the here & now. Anyway, if I can just say this
on what's a rather vast subject, people always turn up
                            everywhere late,
because they can change their beliefs more easily than
                            themselves.
They always know more than they understand. Then
                            suddenly at the least
convenient opportunity what rears its ugly head is their
                            once-dead dreams.
They want to stay children, colour in the book with God in it
                            with coloured crayons
but God turned up incognito & the miracle went &
                            happened some time ago.

5–6 June 1989

Overweight

They say less & less & use more & more perfume.
They need only a quarter of an hour for a night of love.
                              Their feelings are putting on weight.
They have handed their children into the care of the
                              Muppets & the Smurfs.
Above their beds the passionate words: "I will never leave
                              you" hang in touched-up lettering.

They display their feelings embarrassedly like luggage in
                              front of a customs official, as if they were
                              carrying out some harsh penance.
Every evening they escape from their home, her into a
                              fashion catalogue, him into some thriller.
In the mornings they hurry to the factories producing (first
                              and foremost) sadness.
They have a three-year old car, & two illicit affairs each on
              their consciences. It wasn't going to work, was it?

3.5.89

Grass Accepts

The grass accepts the cigarette ends & brown crawly things
thrown out of the tent.
The earth, the largest orphanage in the universe, patiently
tolerates
our childish whims & antics.
Our tears & shooting at each other,
pouring salt into the fruit salad & placing bombs underneath
things.
A strong wind blowing, the tent clutches the earth as tightly
as a child
hangs onto its Mother's hand. I am writing in a horizontal
position, the strength
necessary to understanding this world is rising up through my
stomach.
The blades of grass straining upwards point me in the right
direction. Love,
Love gives us a chance to win through despite our own
being.

Marzena Broda

Marzena Broda was born in Kraków in 1966 and began publishing in 1985. Associated with the 'new wave' of 'Barbarian' poets who publish in the Kraków-based quarterly *brulion,* Broda published *Światło przestrzeni* (The Light of Space) in Kraków in 1990 for which she was awarded the Kazimiera Iłłakowiczówna prize. Some of these poems also appeared in *Przyszli barbarzyńcy.*

A Motif from Brodsky

It was a pure light blue winter's night.
The city's streets lay outside the horizon of human vision.
Everything was lulled beneath a fresh layer of fluff,
shaggy sculptures of stones piled up on the shore
of the abyss by time, forests and roads slumbered,
the moon already deep in sleep in its silvery trailing gown.
The birds fell silent in the fields, the drowsy pictures
fluttered out of the memory summoning up ghosts.
Footprints hurled into the wet snow froze,
fog swirled behind the iced trees.
There was no one, only the falling snow's murmurs,
wind at the foot of an immobile mountain, silent.
Was it hoping for silence?
Human exhalation implausibly attempted to warm the air,
angels played on their trumpets poking through perforations
in the clouds, their tears sparkling like real stars
listing each and every earthbound name.
Everything was becoming dead, dozy and dreamy.
Words disappeared somewhere, wooden houses stood
abandoned,
dawn, stiff with frost, did not appear on the scene.
Valleys solidified, as did light on the slopes,
and mountain waterfalls like the crystals of polar ice fields.
The sun had fallen asleep, as had the days
of an Indian summer, the planets, the cosmos,
as had souls throughout the universe. Somewhere at the
                                        back of thought's
deep space – Snow is falling, time changes guard.
Sleep then, world, fast in the winter's white arms.
Earth's heart beats on gently.

December 1988

Marzena Broda

A House of Red Brick

In this house there were holy things: a photograph spliced
by a black mourning ribbon, a candle melted in a candelabra
after a farewell soirée, a telephone hung up on the wall
midway through some word. Nothing else, perhaps only
loneliness,

whose refuge is damnation.
Wherever we go, it will chaperone us while
pointing the way out of captivity: the same abyss
for everyone. A house as mortal as we are. Wild animals
who devoid of anger throw themselves onto their prey.

*   *   *

Close my eyes, still my voice
and unbind my hands so I may reach out for heaven
only then will I find a way through the boundlessness
that separates us.

I feel the sun sinking, its glow sets
behind the moorlands. What shall become of me?
I shall attain the unknown night and in the homeland of the
                                                                    darkness
I will not discern the road to you.

Close my eyes, still my voice.
If you do not I shall collapse exhausted
by the far flight towards heaven, and then never,
even at your calling will we meet
in this universe that so isolates people from the Gods.

Marzena Broda

Watery World

The ocean has thrown these smooth bones onto the shore
and like splinters off a tree they take root in the sticky
beach.

Pebbles carried off by a wave emit the sound of
castanets. The wind rests in the cloud formations
and shells sparkle beneath the green waters.
There at the bottom clouds emerge from the caves.
– Has someone lit a torch?
Over the top of the coral reefs fish swim
whose universe is the starting point of silence.

1987

Oh, My Love . . .

for M.

When the boisterous wind pulls itself to life
seek refuge beyond the eternal mountain for on Earth
which is round and in fact has but few paths
there is no one to protect you: oh, my love
whatever you are in that heavenly attire
whether dawn sunrise sunset rain that
taps at the closed winter lake Run away
to where roads have no beginning nor end
for in this place the gloom will inexplicably sweep away:
hearing sight stranded fish the smile on a human face
a stream of blood on a cracked palm an incandescent
stone which provides warmth and security Everything

*   *   *

To wake up before the sunrise,
to see the sky's ceiling propped up by a meadow,
a sleepy evening, rocked by a cloud.
To touch, while light still dozes inside the earth
a Tatra mountainscape painted with time's gloss.
To pray for everything, to forget anxieties,
poems, that comfortable armchair in the city,
to make out the stars at night above human habitation,
to hold your face in my hands at the hour
of rest. Oh, if only I could get used to silence!
To hear beech trees wilt and their leaves rust
when scattered over the world's floor.
Blood flows more silently.
The landscape yellows. And rain closes the eyelids.

What Version of Truth Will Survive?

In which days or nights
will we come to face the dead
and always that self-same trace of uncertainty

Will it be necessary to cross hurriedly over
to the other side without taking a breath through sleep
Will swarms of birds fly over us
lazily waking the air with their wings
Will we reach the receding landscape
thus overtaking the future
What truth will survive on the Plains of Eden
Will time exist without us
In what dimension will we leave proof of our existence
to ourselves to the Earth to the stooping tree of love
Will anyone now be able to promise
a similar place in the Unknown
Will the seasons that pass over the steely
green colour of lakes and forests flow after us
Where do all thoughts really lead
the movement of a hand that falls onto a face in anger or
                                                    sorrow

the sounds and silence Light of first dusk
The planet that embraces Giving shelter

Hymn

You who made the myth of the eternal paradise,
before the sun penetrated through to the depths of infinity,
    take a look past your daily grind
    into the cloudy distance of time and light.

On the rim of the gloom your paradisiacal servants
lost, in the silence, their feathers and crashed down into the
                                  sea.
    The earth opened its dry mouth,
    as the moon rose the ruler of the night.

Now he is their lord, chooses dreams,
and acts as silent guide around the ashes of paradise.
    You cannot do much now. Within your cold
    steely heaven, which has no end,
forests, archipelagoes, ravines full of people and torchlight,
music and the seasons have sunk.
    Take pleasure in that truth. While we
    are carried by the white ground down to the bottom
                                  of hell.

There at the bottom is our place, our time
and world, which thanks to your power lies in evil.
    Life flows in it like a river of darkness,
    without regret, suffering or fear
then it suddenly cascades into the abyss of space
and thus it is that if only by brushing against the future with
                            a single word
    we are forever fading, never prepared for your way.

Marcin Sendecki

Marcin Sendecki was born in Gdańsk in 1967. He was a student of medicine from 1986-90, he is currently doing postgraduate work in sociology at the University of Warsaw. He lives outside Warsaw in Tomaszów Lubelski. His debut as poet came in 1987, and he has published in various magazines, and was included in the anthology *przyszli barbarzyńcy* (the barbarians have arrived). His first volume, *Z wysokości* (Looking Down) appeared in the *bibLioteka brulionu* series in 1992.

Certainly

It's certainly still too early, but
when is it likely to start? Certainly not
now, a few minutes before seven, certainly
not here, in this train running on the Warsaw-Lublin line
and maybe not even with these people, with all eight,
including
me, staring out of the window, at their newspapers and into
their neighbours' eyes, although
it is far easier to cross-check their colour by reaching into
handbags or
hearts

1986

Marcin Sendecki

An Old Song

She usually gets back home at three in the morning
I don't even know whether she sleeps on her back, whether
she presses her face deep into the pillow, I just don't know.
                              During the summer
at this time of the morning the birds' chattering in chorus,
                                        men silently
pick up their fishing gear and trek all the way to
the waterside. Now incubation takes pigeons longer,
first snow ploughs scream past scaring the hell,
then a couple of cars mash down grey sludge,
eventually breakfast under the glare of bare light bulbs.
She should wake up soon. When we leave,
I will pass her that overcoat.

1985

July the Twenty-first*

From a bus window: flags gulped up by the wind and
a man in his working clothes, lighting the eternal flame: a
                                              test run: but
the thick smoke is real and softly streams up into the air torn
                                     by the boundaries
of its own limits. We're still here, this side of July where the
                                        wooden language
of government decrees is on its marks to be force-fed and:
                                              right here:
beneath the thin sunlight dripping with sweat, in leather
                                        clothing, with
hands folded – over the back of the neck, down paper
                                        trenches, in open
mouths, into which we vanish raising glasses and voices.
                                              Right here.

*The day before the official holiday that used
to celebrate the foundation of the communist People's Republic

Marcin Sendecki

This Time There Will Be No Injuries

This will be a holiday, sudden and sublime, full of
sunshine and shiny new shoes. This
time megaphones will not let us down, boys will
spit joyously from high balconies and meat, oh, meat
will cruise down streets while we light cigarettes
from flaming torches. And there will be so many words,
clear as copper bells, like the sound of church doors closing.
It will be a holiday, and we will eat
cakes.

1989

Buses and Trams

Newspapers live faster and faster. Now you also
have your place in their mouths, as you read, over
the shoulder of some youngster, some of your own
words. The yellow stills advance, money and
adresses melt in your pockets;

April 1989, Warsaw

Marcin Sendecki

Sunday

My heart is in my pocket
Frank O'Hara

Light smoothly oversteps frontiers of glassiness,
mingles with breath and smoke of cheap cigarettes.
Yellow paint peels off walls, flakes over bedlinen,
stalks of fixtures and fittings, and a table's clear surface. My

                                                             heart
lies before me, inert.

Looking Down

Looking down from the second floor you can see a car park,
                             the narrow towers
of an Orthodox church and scales of plaster on the bodies of
                              tall blocks
shedding their skin, further off, beyond this wall, people
                            move down streets,
swallowing syllables, a ribbon of rainwater tightens around
                            the throat
walking down the staircase you see children run into a
                          pudddle's hoop, beads
of sweat roll down foreheads, and you hear, behind you, the
                          commands shouted
by a seven-year old leader, a little way on you stand still, the
                         umbrella's canvas
when fingered on the inside lets rain through, your wet hair
                         stiffens,
a one-hundred zloty note with Waryński's face on it, hidden
                         inside my jacket, shivers with cold,
you'll spend him in a while, exchanging him for tobacco and
                         matches; as if that
kiosk was the headquarters of the secret police or a bureau
                         de change of the elements:
it's July, and life – put off until some later date – folds up
into a single lump and fits in an inside pocket;

1987

Artur
Szlosarek

Artur Szlosarek was born in 1968, and studies comparative litera-
ture at the University of Bonn, in Germany. Szlosarek made his
debut in the pages of the once-émigré *Zeszyty Literackie* (Literary
Volumes). He has published in numerous other magazines, but his
first volume, *Wiersze napisane* (Written poems) was published by
the Kraków-based *oficyna literacka* in 1991.

Esoterium

a cigarette between my fingers, a sheet of paper lying
                                        crumpled
on the table, a pen-knife rammed into the table-top next to
slowly yellowing books, a junior bicycle's squeal snarled up
                                                in
pleading children's voices, the acrid-smelling skins of bitter
                                            plums,

courage and time are silently confined to their own
                                    preoccupations,
the garnishes and flourishes of smoke, letters read only once,
                                            newspapers
long out of date and put to one side for later reading discuss
at great length in a familiar voice questions of responsibilities
                                            and rights,

and the day lapses into its nadir, and from one poem I read
another poem takes shape, stepping incoherently from one
                                                world
into the next, well what else did you expect, spirit or shadow
pathologically torn apart by its subject, it can protect you,
                                                me,

chroniclers intended little else, unable as they are to codify
the hour-glasses in sequence, so too Ockham's Razor
                                        constantly slips
between their fingers, since on the scale of each of the cities
a cemetery weighs more heavily than a kindergarten,

on a brick wall leaves make their presence felt by the sound
                                            they make
and that is the sole means by which the winds' evil purpose is
                                            revealed,
so Midas, the long-eared king, is still obliged to trust
                                            implicitly
in the good intentions of his personal consultant, the barber

October 1989

Artur Szlosarek

Letter to Xanthippe

who exactly are you, under the long shadow cast by your
                                                                husband –
are you a god-fearing wife, or a woman searching for
satisfaction from the bodies of momentary lovers,

Xanthippe,

they talk of you in various ways: as envious, as proud,
impregnated by an idiot, holding your head up high
(there are as many tongues as people)

Xanthippe,

day and night, your mouth goes numb with the wine's
                                                                dryness
wheaten bread, lemons, grain bursting in clay
vessels, jugfuls of dusty water and a grim smile

Xanthippe,

as you hear the singing of olive sellers (your slowly
circulating blood sustains your consciousness) – do you
                                                                understand
what it is that each person desperately defends,

Xanthippe,

you walk across graves under the sun of your homeland
you burn your feet on the hot stones (your hands submerged
                                                                in the heavens
cannot help you),

Xanthippe,

do you know that you do not know

In Memoriam

Judas Iscariot, now forsaken, it is to you that
I dedicate these few lines in memory of the day
on which – so they say – you were adopted as victim
of inscrutable obscurity for God's master plan,

you must surely have realized the extent of the power
of him to whom the three kings brought gifts
one fine day you accepted an infamous assignment,
thus you became, you fool, a synonym for betrayal –

your history, remarkable as it seems, is familiar to
us all: the feast of passover, a final supper,
a man holding a jug leads you to an ordinary table,
bread crumbs, the smell of pressed grapes,

and with a last caress of your lips the moment came,
our long-awaited power, the riddle, his halo,
spat upon, denigrated, chained – he then abandoned us
one whose doubts were satisfied by their cosmic echo,

hopelessly you considered adding to the torpor of the ox
or splitting the crusted womb with the soundness of an oar,
you fell – just as a dispensible member is amputated,
humbled by time, without cause or consequence

Artur Szlosarek

Errare Humanum Est

your civilization, Slavonic superstitions,
forest divinities, love behind the bushes
or deep in the dark night, books, endless numbers
of kings, princesses unfaithful yet pure,

routes of uncontrolled commerce, of the continuous
exchange of virtues, premonitions, passion and coins,
loaves and tears, dependability and risk, and fortune
spinning round like a wheel, *non omnis moriar*,

routes leading from sea to sea, impassable
roads to be followed, full of desire, dust,
sand, between the place of birth, and life, and
the end, and between heaven and earth, leather

wine-skins brimming with fermented fruit,
baskets of flowers and ornaments, all that renders
beauty brighter and elevates what is ugly,
everything that you can hold and feel,

carefully staggering figures, shadows
shifting from one town to the next,
guides tasting the sand, the blind
with a knowledge of destiny, majesty and pride,

Jews whisper the kaddish to one another, Muslims
face Eastwards, Jesuits make the sign of
the cross, wise men from distant lands
their gaze fixed on themselves, and animals,

terrified slaves, Romans, connoisseurs
of the fairer sex and legal distinctions, thieves,
shamen, artists and your own faith, mission
and constancy, on any and this occasion:

an archetype bursting with its lust for this world, a fairy tale
left to its own devices, lips that retell every moment

ever experienced, hands unable to commit to memory
the features of a person's face, incapable of challenging,

avoiding or defining

*   *   *

take no notice of me, hand, that
lends a fidgety presence to
clay vessels – your
prestidigitation, so beautiful and brimming with
extraordinary gesticulation, points to
us, obliviously immersed in ourselves,
when suddenly we feel joy, yes, and
that underhand and proud summary of
non-existence, a predictable
coldness in your clammy
grip, in its crystal sweat

Reflection

there is one basic question that preys on my mind
so today (18 June 1991) I shall attempt to
pin it down: whether in fact it is possible
to say anything sincere from the heart
here, now, after all else has been said –

I doubt that, though not entirely, since
perhaps I am just asking the wrong question:
because it may well be the case that what I do know
from the printed matter of my own age is
only the appendix or supplement,

though if it is just a marginal scribble, what about the text
it is interpreting: whose thoughts does it summarize,
or comment on– certainly culture operates
on the basis of a palimpsest, but now
the obvious question: who erases the original text

theologians give the shortest answer, biologists
delve into the genetic code, but pain and uncertainty
find refuge in the former and the latter:
are these their specificities or do they mutate
endlessly like the conscience or the butterfly,

nature either engrosses or bewilders us
there is nothing new in it besides the records
of ancient times and its malevolent evolutions –
the wandering spider avoids the wild strawberry
clinging to the ground as anyone can see

should they want to or take the opportunity

*   *   *

at any stage you can make a fresh start: maybe
you can't hear the birds of paradise whose screeching pierces
your eardrums and the air, but they exist
forever, as you do

at any stage you can make a fresh start: maybe
you can't sense how overwhelming the respiration of plants

is,

how the shadows of insects pass back and forth within
the heavy sweetness of flowers

at any stage you can make a fresh start: maybe
you don't recall that moaning of animals,
the taste of springs or person predestined for you, or why
you refresh your feet at the waterside

at any stage you can make a fresh start: maybe
you just don't know that you carry so very much inside you
and the instant you hold out your hand you become,

momentarily:

the star Wormwood,

and the chewed apple rolls past

Paweł Marcinkiewicz

Paweł Marcinkiewicz was born in 1969 in Opole. From 1990 he was a student of English Literature at the University of Wrocław, and now teaches English in a local primary school. So far he has published three slim volumes: *Zostaw noc niech płynie* (Leave the Night Let It Flow On, published by *Wolność i Pokój,* Opole, 1988), *Uciekaj Macinkiewic Uciekaj* (Run Macinkiewicz Run, Warsaw 1990) and *18 wierszy o tym, że ogień będzie różą* (18 Poems on the Fact that Fire Will Be a Rose, in the Okolice series, 1991). His poetry has also been presented in magazines like *Na Głos.*

Poem for Marcus Aurelius

"Will you too, my soul, one day be good,
simple, unique, bare, more visible, than
this body which has trapped you?"
Marcus Aurelius, Meditations X, 1

To make use of the hundreds of kilometres travelled by
train,
Of cigarettes smoked on an empty stomach, or bridges,
aching muscles,
of what is continually put off till tomorrow, till never, lost
between
a glass and raising it to your lips; to fall in love with want and
tame the
view from the window; to carry the sky's outstretched shirt
like a banner;
then to discard contempt, to drown the torches of anger and
to speak
of one's persecutors without hissing consonants; not to count
the days, not to fear
labyrinths or chasms; and not to envy the life span of sequioa
trees,
or the freedom of the stars; and as for snorted out words
"get to fuck . . ." heard in a doorway –
to feel love; to be able not to have, to not claim greater
poverty than someone suffering:

This we cannot manage. We collect stamps and saliva and we
are rarely upset
By camps or prison cells in other countries; the only thing
that unites us with our friends
or enemies is our fear, our trembling at the dictatorship
Of blood cells, of gas chambers; our throats always repeat
that same
Incantation: "Be good to me, Planet of the Murderers,
Planet of the
Hyenas"; we sleep badly, we slip dust into our drinks – fire
has rented out

The windows of our senses and words; we would like to
                          scream, that this isn't quite right . . .
That the kingdom . . . that the resurrection of the body . . .
                       that our souls . . . that it was granted
To us by the Almighty – but we wade through enormous
                       rooms, down corridors where
All the doors are firmly locked. We stand alone in front of
                       the firing squad.

Escape from Byzantium

> *That is no country for old men*
> W.B. Yeats

I

That is no country for people. The land of nettles
black with longing, of small towns, where beating their
hands against the glass – daylight is welcomed, the innocent
                                        exclamation:
"O, Satan!" – enraptures nuns,
Baracco – bares his fangs. You are like the small boy
who fell asleep in the sick flower – the tempter
paints you a throne, a palace, the pure blue of a river . . .
Oh, Isaac. It's a dream. Open your eyes.

II

Then I shall build a ship – me – the foolish
Ulysses condemned by Ithaca
to the life of a pharmacist – ridiculous defeats,
meagre victories, the fine sand of songs:
We are the soap people – each of us longs
for colours, storms, battles, the crunching of cold skulls."
That is why I shall escape setting sail by sea
From the holy city of Byzantium.

III

Once upon a time there was a country far away: in it there
were   trains filled
with loaves of bread – high above the trains there sang.
An aeroplane, an angel danced, the moon
hung out its full phase under the sky's eyelashes.
No one knew the tales of the soldier's helmet,
or of the flood. The woodcutters trembled about the trees.
Whatever the men touched did indeed turn to
gold – so pure that it was unreal.

IV

Sails like the wings of dead dragonflies. It is possible
to pour from one bowl into another or gin down one's
$$\text{throat,}$$
or gawk at the grapefruit-like sea griffin.
On the left is the isle of Utopia – with its attractive
torture tower. On the right is Scylla – the god-fearing –
Fish . . . Somehow I just have no desire to disembark . . .
$$\text{It's sultry . . .}$$
I shall sail on. Somewhere there is the end of this lullaby
woven from these waves . . . Glinting . . . Choirs . . .
$$\text{Thunder voicing: "Sancti!"}$$

The Expedition of Macinkiewic, Knight Errant

Macinkiewic made up his mind to become
a Knight Errant.

He could no longer stand
the News he got from the World or Children's Newsround.

– How can you not stand up against evil?
– Shreder must surrender!
This he says quietly to himself.

He, Macinkiewic, will save this world:
So he puts on his Helmet named Mambrina,
and in his shiny armour he mounts his Rosinante.

He is about to grab the spear into his hand
and holding on fast to his saddle
he crosses the verges of the motorways,
and the passable bridges.

He passes by the fortress chimneys of the factories.
Nothing turns him back:
He plunges his sword into the hosts of pedestrians or Moors,
he tramples down the regiments of Lorry-Giants.

He occupies the railway castles,
throwing armies to their knees.

Liberated from their tormentors, not surprisingly, the
                                                    innocent
faint on seeing his courageous countenance.

– Well I'll set off tomorrow.
– I'll certainly get going then.
He says quietly to himself.

240

And he looks out of the window
as the formless clouds advance on the city
and instead of stars car headlights begin to twinkle.

1992

*   *   *

The night is so dark – and you have inside you
A river where the trout sparkle, a butterfly
Flies so high that he could be a star.
Even when bereft of the right words I describe
The earth's hunger as you walk upon it, its rapture
When for you the firmament turns pure blue.
If the world is a sonnet – then you are
Its rhyme, rhythm and stanza.
You are water's pause, fire's exclamation
Mark – if this world is only the world.
You have within you a sound so clear it could
Be called death –beyond the frontiers
      Of language I will carry you in my blood – for I
      Am a castaway on the raft of the pronoun 'You'.

Lullaby

Sleep now. The fire brigade and a glass of water are keeping
watch
Over you. The floor will not give way and this bed will not
fold into the heart
Of fear kidnapped by the fire. Close your eyes. The cord of
the light bulb
Will not burn you, neither will the ceiling's whiteness. Sleep

Soundly. Your blood will not burst into flames. No burning
will overcome you.
The fire will not engulf the bedclothes. It will not force its
way into the lungs
Through your nostrils. Sleep soundly. The darkness will not
commit arson.
You will not run flaming like a torch. The fire

Will not eat away at your face or arms. There will be no war
Of flaming rags. Sleep now. You will have an uneventful
sleep. No escaping from the burning wall to the edge

Of the sheet. No bandages. The fire will not creep
Under your eyelids. Sleep deeply. You will not cry out in
flames.
Sleep now. The flame cannot wake you. Not even a flame
can wake you.

Tomasz
Titkow

Tomasz Titkow was born in Warsaw in 1969, where he has been studying psychology. His first volume of poetry and literary debut was published at his own cost in Warsaw in 1990, entitled *Komu dzwoni budzik* (For Whom the Alarm Clock Rings).

*   *   *

the life I lead's not up to much
I'm in a comfortable situation
my dinners get cooked for me
floors get waxed
from time to time
I get wrecked and get all optimistic
I get surprised at things
though nothing too heavy of course
and I swallow loads of aspirin
when 'flu rages round me

sometimes
I lock the doors and windows
and on a piece of rather naff paper
I try if I can
to save myself from oblivion
which
quite frankly
isn't that easy for me

Tomasz Titkow

O, You Wonderful World!

O, you wonderful world!
you really don't take me seriously enough

you don't ever challenge my bravery
or even my sense of honour
no lions' jaws or swans' hearts
no chance of snide remarks when facing my executioner
at best I get these ridiculous doubts
which I can only laugh at afterwards
as I welcome in the new day by brushing my teeth

my words
try as hard as they can
but they're not particularly good at this
they get all tongue-tied
explaining themselves
in a rather unconvincing way
they'll probably soon
take to the bottle

Paternursal Overcare

on his face he had edifickashun etched
an' in his hand he had the Evening Post

thought-wise with him it kinda varied
kinda shitty really

so they took the bus, right

an', sonny, suddenly like, belched all uncouth
– well, it caused a bit of agitashun alright
dad's right there with a bonk on the conk
an' Mars-like dad's nozzle twitches for more
an' just as the next bonk's on its way
sonny jumps up like fuck
and hey, man! reaches right down into his pocket
and pulls out a bag and in it, yeah . . .
 . . . well, in the bag he's stashed four grenades, right!
so he lobs 'em right at dad, who's mad

o, grenades – super spades!

and blat
bang
boom
dad gets blasted high into the sky
and, well, he's no longer of this world
 . . . so sonny keeps on truckin'
humming happily: dee dee dee da
'cos that's off his chest now, ma

Tomasz Titkow

Song of the Night Porter

listen here, you headache you
you just ain't letting me snooze
though I gotta admit that isn't the point
open-eye's what they pay me for

'cause I'm the nigh-nigh-night
porter, yeah – so let me
tell you who I am

sitting here growing stubble on my chin
saving hotel guests from the whores outside
though when mr policeman comes snooping
I play stupid, what d'y'know

I got to go now, 'cause someone's emerged
from the depths of the pitch-black night
so it's time again to put on the stern face
of the one and only intransigent night porter

*   *   *

look, don't you think, dear friend,
that perhaps we take our magnificent obsessions
those carefully nursed hang-ups
too seriously, we agree too easily that
life bores us – just think about it: when it
comes down to it we've made no particular
effort and all we've got to offer is
some complaints, which you'll
admit are pretty out of place here

under the wing of good old Mother Night
we dream endless stories of sweet victory
which in fact we managed to do quite well

just take a look at our unloved brothers
and sisters, at those friends who
we once left to their own devices
look at them and remember their faces and voices
they will rush forward on collision course for life
which really is a lavish feast

we will remain in our slowly more
poisonous hermitages all by ourselves
and with what's left of the wine and if nothing else
we can drink to our own health

*   *   *

and what about you?
aren't you infected by the hunger to break away,
suddenly and unexpectedly
when the only thing you keep with you
is hardness of heart and that smile
slightly distorting the corners of your mouth
when pride's fine madness strangles you
and stops you explaining yourself
or wanting reassurance
as you utter that oh, so sweet word – adieu –
so then you turn your back on everything
and all that is important is
exactly when you start your journey
so tell me –
aren't you infected by the hunger to break away

* * *

in the corner of my bathroom
demons lurk and skulk

did I dye my sideburns black this morning?

she died in my room
that fly
passed on but not entirely gone

four legs sticking right up

I'll arrange her funeral
in the geranium plant pot
and ponder
where her soul is now

     I'll have red cabbage
     salad for supper later

it's great really great
the whole of the universe in my own room

*   *   *

welcome in, shadow
I receive you into
and over myself

I will no longer be this world's devoted admirer
the repository of its abuse and confidences
I will stop getting as drunk on life as
I do on wine

I can only nod my head in understanding

I am frigid inside
and have left you all far behind

I catch hold of the sounds of living
through the walls through the night
from parties at my friends'
from the city's breathing from tales told by
the rain
from the kitchen where mother is washing up
after supper
          – but that's already a dream now
that's a dream now

nothing ever comes back again

only words do
they rain down hard against me
like stones

Other Polish Titles
Published by Forest Books

ARIADNE'S THREAD

Polish Women Poets

~~translated by Susan Bassnett and Piotr Kuhiwczak~~

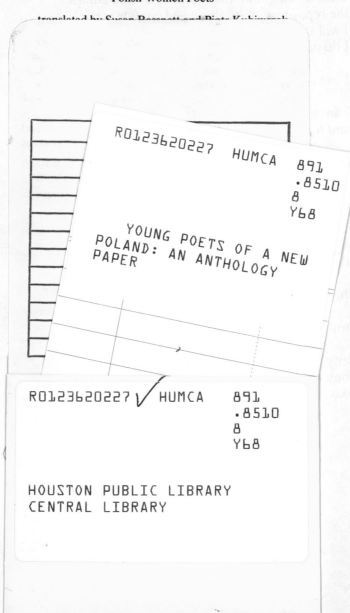